Leon Trotsky

Titles in the series Critical Lives present the work of leading cultural figures of the modern period. Each book explores the life of the artist, writer, philosopher or architect in question and relates it to their major works.

In the same series

Leon Trotsky

Paul Le Blanc

REAKTION BOOKS

This book is dedicated
to the memory of George Breitman

Published by Reaktion Books Ltd
33 Great Sutton Street
London EC1V 0DX, UK
www.reaktionbooks.co.uk

First published 2015
Copyright © Paul Le Blanc 2015

Printed and bound in Great Britain
by Bell & Bain, Glasgow

A catalogue record for this book is available from the British Library

ISBN 978 1 78023 430 4

Contents

Introducing a Life

'A son of a bitch, but the greatest Jew since Jesus Christ' is how Trotsky was described by Raymond Robins, a Teddy Roosevelt Progressive and representative of the American Red Cross in Petrograd. It was late 1917, shortly after the Bolshevik Revolution in Russia inaugurated the birth of modern Communism. Robins was involved in frustrating, fascinating negotiations with Trotsky, who was second only to Vladimir Ilyich Lenin among Russia's revolutionary Marxist leaders.[1]

The actual name of the man was Lev Davidovich Bronstein, but most of the world has known him by his revolutionary nom de plume. Twenty-three years later, an agent of the Communist regime that Trotsky had helped to establish would plunge an alpine ice axe into his head. The assassin – after serving a twenty-year prison sentence in Mexico – travelled to the Union of Soviet Socialist Republics and was awarded the Order of Lenin.

Since his martyrdom in 1940, it can be said that Trotsky has experienced an ongoing resurrection, with well over a dozen biographies and continuing publication of his major writings. Restricting ourselves to the English language, in the past two decades no fewer than ten book-length studies of Trotsky's life and ideas have appeared. If we include studies in which he and his ideas figure prominently, plus novels, songs, poems, plays and both documentary and non-documentary films, then there is the equivalent of a significant work every six months, reflecting

A Russian Civil War poster by Victor Deni, with Trotsky as a revolutionary St George, slaying the dragon of capitalism.

the impact he had on the history of the twentieth century, which continues to reverberate down to our own time.

For millions of people throughout the world, Leon Trotsky was initially seen as a revolutionary liberator. Bertrand Patenaude, one of the more careful critics among his recent biographers, notes that Trotsky – winning over 'vast crowds of workers, soldiers, and sailors in Petrograd with his spellbinding oratory' in 1917 – 'proved to be Lenin's most important ally when the Bolsheviks stormed to power in the October Revolution'. Trotsky himself, in his history of Russia's Revolution, placed emphasis on the multitudes: 'The history of a revolution is for us first of all a history of the forcible entrance of the masses into the realm of rulership over their own destiny.'[2]

He elaborated on this to a radical journalist from the United States, John Reed, in an interview just before the Bolshevik insurrection. The Bolshevik slogan was 'all power to the Soviets', the democratic councils that had sprung up in the revolutionary upsurges of 1905 and again in 1917. 'The Soviets are the most perfect representatives of the people – perfect in their revolutionary experience, in their ideas and objects', Trotsky explained. 'Based directly upon the army in the trenches, the workers in the factories, and the peasants in the fields, they are the backbone of the Revolution.'[3]

Locating the Person

In *Trotsky: A Graphic Biography*, Rick Geary summarizes the story in the first four frames:

> In 1917, Leon Trotsky burst upon the international stage as the brain behind the Russian Revolution. He presided over the complete transformation of his country, not merely a change of government but a total restructuring of society on every level. To many, he was the heroic St George, slaying the dragon of capitalist repression. To others, he was the ruthless and Satanic purveyor of bloody rebellion, the cold, detached theorist gone mad with power. In truth, he fitted neither of these images. He was a writer, a thinker, a nation-builder – albeit a reluctant one – with deep roots in his Russia's agricultural heartland. Trotsky's dream was for a world free from injustice, inequality,

and war, and in this he was absolutely single-minded. To him, the ideas of Karl Marx showed the way, and for one brief moment he set the machinery in motion to achieve that end . . . He lived to see his work betrayed and his ideals perverted by those who seized power after him. He would be ejected from the government he helped to establish and hounded into exile and death.[4]

Some would say this is far too generous. Dmitri Volkogonov insists: 'It was Trotsky's fate that he was able to synthesize an unbending faith in Communist ideals with the mercilessness of the dictatorship of the proletariat, that he could be both one of the inspirers of the Red Terror and its victim.' Another hostile biographer, Robert Service, tells us he was comparable to one of the worst tyrants in the history of the world – 'he was no more likely than Stalin [Lenin's brutal successor] to create a society of humanitarian socialism even though he claimed and assumed he would.'[5] Joshua Rubenstein, in a more generous account, comes to a similar conclusion:

We are left with a compelling image of a ruthless revolutionary, a brilliant journalist, an eloquent historian and pamphleteer, who never softened his faith in dogmatic Marxism, never questioned the need to use violent coercion as an instrument of historical progress, never wondered whether his dream of a proletarian dictatorship could really be the answer to every political, economic, and social failing.[6]

Contrast this with the comment of Max Eastman, who had seen Stalin and Lenin in action and who knew Trotsky personally: 'Lenin combined intellect and idealism with a mastery of the craft of politics. Trotsky inherited the intellect and idealism, Stalin the craft – a fatal split.' Yet he helped shape the world's first Communist regime, organizing and leading to victory the

Lenin and Trotsky amid a throng of workers rallying to the Soviet Republic, 1920.

Red Army in the brutal years of the Russian Civil War (1918–21) –
presenting us with 'a Trotsky who knew how to be hard, to exercise
terror, and a Trotsky fully ready to accept the task of reconstructing
daily life', as Slavoj Žižek has said. Peter Beilharz makes a similar
point with great distaste: Trotsky personified 'the Jacobin legacy',
which 'seeks to improve humanity but kills people'. This is
precisely where one must look to comprehend the real Trotsky,
according to Geoffrey Swain, who is definitely not inclined toward
hero worship: 'By focusing on the years in power, a rather different
picture of Trotsky emerges to that traditionally drawn, more of the
man and less of the myth.'[7]

The present biography is guided by a different conception.
To understand the man, we must, of course, look at his *entire* life –
but in some ways the most decisive qualities of this revolutionary
are to be found in the Trotsky who, in order to remain true to
the ideals that animated his entire life, followed a trajectory that
took him out of the centre of power. This was the doomed but

determined fighter who sought to defend and explain the relevance of the heroic best that was in the early Communist tradition. He expended immense energy to place recent revolutionary experience – including achievements, mistakes, and failures – into perspective, and to use such insights for analysing and battling global crises, new totalitarianisms and the deepening violence that engulfed humanity from 1929 to 1940.

Our focus here will be on this final phase of Trotsky's life. 'The work in which I am engaged now', he asserted in a diary of this exile period, 'despite its extremely insufficient and fragmentary nature, is the most important work of my life – more important than 1917, more important than the period of the Civil War or any other.'[8] Given the existence and role of Lenin and the internal strength of the party that he led, the revolutionary cause would have advanced in earlier periods without Trotsky's existence. But now Lenin and his revolutionary party no longer existed. And the broader revolutionary current, once a powerful force in the international workers' movement, was gone – overwhelmed not only by the onslaughts of fascism and imperialism, but especially by the bureaucratization and disorienting, demoralizing, debilitating corruptions represented by Stalinism and Social-Democratic reformism. Trotsky was labouring to provide historical knowledge, theoretical insights and other political resources that new generations of activists could use to rebuild the necessary revolutionary alternative.

Of course, Trotsky himself would insist on a continuity between the exile and the intransigent revolutionary of earlier years. Beilharz compares him with the Jacobin Robespierre, who inaugurated the Reign of Terror during the French Revolution, intoning: 'I know of only two parties – good citizens and bad citizens.' Beilharz drives home the point: 'Trotsky's defense of revolutionary terror in the Russian Revolution introduces the notion of . . . good and bad citizens, or at least good and bad classes; terrorism toward the latter is historically and politically necessary, therefore proper.' Yet the blurring together of 'citizen' and 'class' suggests that Beilharz's analogy relies more on rhetorical flourish than analysis: unpacking the differences between the two terms, and the meaning of this difference, shows that Trotsky is saying something fundamentally different from Robespierre. Far more interesting is the contention of Žižek: 'The figure of Trotsky . . . remains crucial in so far as it disturbs the alternative "either (social) democratic socialism or Stalinist totalitarianism": what we find in Trotsky, in his writings and his revolutionary practice in the early years of the Soviet Union, is revolutionary terror, party rule, etc., but *in a different mode* from that of Stalinism.'[9] It could be said that the explanation of this point, in ways that can help guide future revolutionary actions, is what Trotsky saw as his fundamental task during the years of his final exile.

In this period Trotsky produced his greatest literary works, including *My Life*, *The History of the Russian Revolution* and *The Revolution Betrayed*, as well as his unfinished biographies of Lenin and Stalin. There was also a steady stream of shorter works, filling more than fourteen volumes. A year-long 'internal exile' within the USSR, in Alma-Ata, was soon followed by three and a half fruitful years in Turkey, short and difficult stints in France and Norway, and finally three vibrant years in Mexico. In all of these places he met with many comrades and co-thinkers, and corresponded with many more who were urgently attempting to build a current in the labour and socialist movements that could contribute positively and effectively in struggles against capitalism and imperialism, against fascism and Nazism, against Stalinism and for the liberation of all people.

A key dimension of Trotsky's reputation is as a brilliantly innovative theorist. In looking at the ideas Trotsky put forward in his theoretical writings, however, I will be inclined to emphasize the aspects of *unoriginality* in Trotsky's thought, especially in

Diego Rivera's mural of 1932 connects Trotsky with Marx and Engels, the Socialist International's revolutionary wing (Rosa Luxemburg and Karl Liebknecht), and the Communist International that he and Lenin had established. Also shown are Left Oppositionist Christian Rakovsky, u.s. Trotskyists James P. Cannon, Max Shachtman and Arne Swabeck, and activists' children.

relation to the much-vaunted theory of permanent revolution, his analysis of Stalinism, his prescriptions for defeating Hitler and the much misunderstood *Transitional Program*. All these are drawn from Marx and from revolutionary Marxists of Trotsky's own time, including the best of Second International Marxism in the period leading up to 1914, as well as the collective project of the early Third International. Trotsky never pretended otherwise, which is why questions of Marxism must necessarily be interwoven into any serious study of Trotsky. His distinctiveness is that, unlike many, he sought to remain true to the old revolutionary perspectives, and in a sense became original simply through applying old principles – as consistently and creatively as he could – to new realities.

Was Trotsky a Liar?

A common accusation has been that Trotsky was motivated by lust for power or vanity, that all his brilliant theorizing is little more than either (a) a weapon to advance his ability to lord it over others in the revolutionary movement and in the new Soviet state, or (b) a set of flourishes, embellishments and rationalizations designed to enhance his reputation. Among the more recent critical biographical studies – by Robert Service, Ian Thatcher and Geoffrey Swain – one finds an inclination to 'break new ground' by arguing precisely along such lines, challenging the interpretations of Trotsky and those taking him seriously.

Swain, Thatcher and Service are not in agreement on all matters. For example, Service dismisses *The History of the Russian Revolution* as a 'mixture of tub-thumping and slipperiness'. On the other hand, Thatcher insists that Trotsky's classic 'still forms our research agenda of the Russian Revolution.' He goes further: 'Measured against *The History of the Russian Revolution* most "modern" research does not seem so "modern" after all. Any student of 1917 would be foolish to overlook *The History of the Russian Revolution*.'[10]

On the other hand, Thatcher complains that Trotsky's account of his role in the 1905 and 1917 revolutions, and in the Russian Civil War, is inflated. This should not be surprising, given that, according to Thatcher, 'there was little evidence of conscientiousness in Trotsky's work habits.' He concludes that 'whatever the qualities of Trotsky's leadership [in the Russian Civil War], one can throw doubt on its significance by arguing that the fundamental causes of the Red victory lay elsewhere.' He cites Geoffrey Swain to support this point, but Swain himself (on the basis of a more careful study of primary sources than is evident in Thatcher) actually insists that 'Trotsky was an inspirational organizer', and that 'without Trotsky there would have been no October Revolution and no Bolshevik victory in the Russian civil war.'[11]

Yet there is also much that unites these authors, including a tendency to converge around the sort of things Swain presents in his study: Trotsky's own writings are unreliable; Lenin and Trotsky had entirely different visions of the 1917 insurrection; Trotsky was not viewed by Lenin as his heir; Trotsky, far from being an internationalist, firmly believed in the possibility of building socialism in one country, just as Stalin did.[12]

The balance of serious scholarly opinion – whether one considers older studies by Isaac Deutscher, E. H. Carr and Moshe Lewin, or more recent and diverse works by Bruce Lincoln, Richard B. Day, Ronald Suny, David Mandel, Daniel Gaido, John Marot and Thomas Twiss – remains tilted in a different direction from this. Despite well-documented and commonly acknowledged tactical differences, Lenin and Trotsky in 1917 (according to these scholars) shared the same basic vision of revolutionary worker-peasant insurrection, led by the Bolsheviks and working through the democratic councils, or soviets. This balance of opinion also tilts toward the view that Lenin's desired 'heir' would have been a collective leadership in which Trotsky would play an important role and within which Stalin would be dramatically demoted (if not removed). And it acknowledges the centrality of Trotsky's revolutionary internationalism.

It can certainly be documented that Trotsky worked tirelessly, after the 1917 Revolution (and particularly in the 1920s), to help build up and develop the economy of the Soviet Republic, and that he explicitly, consistently and energetically sought to do this in a manner that would contribute to the country's development in a socialist direction. Yet it can also be documented that Trotsky explicitly and consistently (and at times *more* than some other Bolsheviks) argued that the fate of the Russian Revolution was dependent on the spread of victorious working-class revolutions to other countries, especially in Europe, but also beyond. This was one of the central themes in Trotsky's theory of permanent revolution as it evolved in 1904–6. This was – Lenin and Trotsky agreed – one of the reasons why Marxists could and should have risked a revolution in the Russia of 1917 in the first place. That was the purpose for devoting such immense time, energy and resources to organizing and developing the Communist International from 1919 through 1922 and beyond – to help build revolutionary parties throughout the world that would be capable of leading the planet's labouring majorities in replacing capitalism with socialism. (When Stalin and those around him abandoned that perspective, with the notion that socialism could be established in their own single country, the degeneration of the Communist International as a revolutionary body naturally unfolded, culminating in its 'twilight' in 1935 and its dissolution in 1943.)[13]

As Service, Thatcher and Swain all emphasize, their 'innovations' fly in the face of what Trotsky himself insists upon in his autobiography and many other writings. Which naturally raises the question· was Trotsky lying?

Swain definitely does not see Trotsky as a simple liar, inclining to the view that instead he 'was willfully seeing what he wanted to see, blinded by the passion of debate'. A similar picture emerges from Thatcher's *Trotsky*. 'Given recent events, his autobiography could be nothing other than polemical', writes Thatcher. 'It was an opportunity to defend himself and attack others, along lines set by the debates and accusations of the internal party wrangles of the 1920s.' He notes: 'Trotsky was aware of this and made no attempt to hide this fact from his readers.' Thatcher's criticisms of *My Life* are revealing:

> It draws upon sources in a highly selective manner, taking care to refer only to those that confirm the author's view of events . . . Trotsky is careful to show his concern for historical truth . . .

[and] at several points . . . refers to documents kept secret in the USSR because of praise for Trotsky contained in them. However, Trotsky does not confront the possibility that he also used the past for political purposes.[14]

From this one might expect rationalizations and evasions from Trotsky, not to mention superficial or mistaken judgements. There were also times, to be sure, when he did *not* tell the truth: in efforts to shield the Opposition from Stalin's attacks, he would issue public denials in the mid-1920s about the existence of Lenin's 'testament' that had been revealed by Max Eastman, and in the 1930s he covered up certain contacts with dissident Communists in the USSR. The fact remains that his major writings did not contain blatant falsehoods, conscious lies or the fabrication of documents. Yet this is precisely what would have to be the case, in such works as *My Life* and *The History of the Russian Revolution*, if we were to accept some of the 'innovative' interpretations. While historical controversies will naturally continue, if Trotsky actually *thinks* he is telling the truth, then some of the new interpretations are implausible, especially if his account is consistent with various primary and secondary sources.

Personality and Ideology

What Trotsky *thinks* he is trying to do obviously brings us to the question of the personality of the man we are considering. One of the most interesting pen portraits comes from one who knew him well over a period of years, Anatoly Lunacharsky, who first met Trotsky at the start of the 1905 revolutionary upsurge. 'Trotsky was then unusually elegant, unlike the rest of us, and very handsome', Lunacharsky remembers. 'This elegance and his nonchalant, condescending manner of talking to people, no

Creator of the Red Army with wartime comrades.

matter who they were, gave me an unpleasant shock.' Of course, in this period, Trotsky was aligned with the Menshevik faction of the Russian socialist movement and Lunacharsky was a partisan of Lenin's Bolsheviks. Within a few months, Lunacharsky's perception shifted when Trotsky matured as a leader of the powerful democratic workers' council (or soviet) of St Petersburg amid the revolutionary upsurge that was challenging the Russian monarchy. Lunacharsky records that Lenin's face initially darkened upon hearing of Trotsky's rise to the leadership of the soviet, but then commented: 'Well, Trotsky has earned it by his brilliant and unflagging work.'[15] Indeed, Trotsky's capacity for collective functioning, for comradely teamwork, would show itself not only in 1905, but recurrently at key moments – in the revolutionary events of 1917, in organizing the Red Army, in oppositional efforts of the 1920s and often in the work of the Fourth International in the 1930s. Such capacity for political collaboration stood in striking contrast to the personal prickliness which some who knew him noted more than once.

Trotsky's immersion in the radical workers' movement had provided the fire and the glow of his life since his eighteenth year, when he and other young activists – primarily students – became involved in agitational and educational efforts among the inhabitants of industrial Nikolaev. Some of the workers were animated by subversively radical forms of Christianity and by the early beginnings of trade unionism, and the revolutionary students learned as much as they taught. Trotsky later recalled:

The workers streamed toward us as if they had been waiting for this. They all brought friends; some came with their wives, and a few older men joined the groups with their sons. We never sought them out; they looked for us. Young and inexperienced leaders that we were, we were soon overwhelmed by the movement we had started. Every word of ours met with a response. As many as twenty and twenty-five or more of the workers gathered at our secret readings and discussions, held in houses, in the woods, or on the river.[16]

Twenty years later he still recalled the names of the militant workers to whom he had brought the revolutionary gospel, and who had taught him so much – Mukhin, Korotkov, Savelyevitch, Yefimov, Babenko. Years later he was still sharing with younger comrades some of the lessons he had learned in the workers' districts of Nikolaev – for example, that 'intellectuals and half-intellectuals' should not 'terrorize the workers by some abstract generalities and paralyze the will toward activity', but instead

Nineteen-year-old Lev Bronstein, seated at the right, with three revolutionary comrades in Odessa – Grigori Sokolovsky, G. A. Ziv and Alexandra Sokolovskaya, who introduced him to Marxism and became his first wife.

'should have in the first place a good ear, and only in the second place a good tongue'.[17] Largely through such interactive immersion, Trotsky found his own voice. 'I could sense the glory and pathos of the Revolution', the u.s. journalist William Reswick, who knew Russian, remembered from one of Trotsky's speeches in 1926, although similar accounts can be found from 1905, 1917 and the Civil War years. 'He was a virtuoso of speech, a master of oratory who could play on the heartstrings of men with the ease and grace of a violinist. In a few minutes he had the crowd hypnotized. They cheered, laughed, cried, responding to the speaker's every mood and gesture.' But the rapture flowed both ways. 'We found the workers more susceptible to revolutionary propaganda than we had ever in our wildest dreams imagined', Trotsky recalled of the early days in Nikolaev. 'The amazing effectiveness of our work fairly intoxicated us.' In addition Trotsky helped to produce revolutionary literature (and soon gained the nickname *Pero* – 'the pen'), and recalled 'what a satisfied feeling I had when I received the information from mills and workshops that the workers read voraciously' the handbills and newspapers in which he wrote about their plight and urged resistance to oppressive realities.[18]

Trotsky later confessed that he had not read a single revolutionary book in his earliest activist years, becoming acquainted with the *Communist Manifesto* only by reading it and explaining it in workers' study circles. Yet the revolutionary activist milieu in which Trotsky participated was ideologically heterogeneous. Trotsky himself was at the time a radical populist, vociferously rejecting Marxism as a 'dogmatic' doctrine. He mocked the most prominent Marxist in the group, Alexandra Sokolovskaya. 'You still think you're a Marxist?' he exclaimed. 'I can't imagine how a young girl so full of life can stand that dry, narrow, impractical stuff!' She shot back: 'I can't imagine how a person who thinks he is logical can be contented with a headful of vague, idealistic emotions!' Within a short time, Trotsky and

Alexandra were involved in a relationship and a short-lived marriage that after 1902 gave way to a lifelong but long-distance friendship. More durably, Trotsky became a committed Marxist.[19]

'To follow the evolution of Marx's thought, to experience its irresistible force upon oneself, to discover under introductory sentences or notes lateral galleries of conclusions, to become convinced over and over of the aptness and depth of his sarcasm, and to bow in gratitude before a genius who has been merciless to himself became . . . not only a necessity, but a delight.'[20] In this passage from his biography of the young Lenin, Trotsky was also writing about himself.

With a grand philosophical sweep that comprehends reality as an evolving and dynamic interplay of matter and energy, Marxism projects reality as a vibrant totality in which amazing qualities of humanity (creative labour, community, the quest for freedom) have generated technological advances, economic surpluses and consequent inequalities that – in turn – generate struggles against oppression. This way of seeing history perceived a succession of economic systems nurturing different social structures and cultures. Since the rise of civilization, all the social-economic systems (whether ancient slave civilizations, feudalism or capitalism) have involved powerful minorities who have been enriched by the exploitation of labouring majorities. But sometimes the oppressed labourers fight for a better life – more food, genuine community, freedom – with their exploiters striving to keep them in their place.[21]

While the history of global civilization has been marked by such class struggles, capitalism is unique, generating technological innovations and spectacular increases in productivity, producing enough wealth – ultimately – to provide a decent life for all people, if only the economy could be made the common property of all. Capitalism's distinctive economic expansionism naturally transforms a majority of the people into workers, who can make a living only through selling their ability to work (labour-power) for payment from the capitalist employer, but whose labour creates the actual wealth that makes society possible and whose life-activity allows for the functioning of society.

Marxists naturally see this working class as being the key to creating a socialist future. The working-class majority must organize to make it so: build large, inclusive trade unions for better wages and working conditions; build powerful social movements to bring changes for the better (reforms); build the political power of the working-class majority 'to win the battle of democracy'; and bring about a transition from capitalism to socialism (which they saw as the extension of 'rule by the people' – democracy – over society's economic life, providing for the dignity and free development of all).

For Trotsky, the revolutionary struggle fused with this revolutionary ideology of Marxism, and both blended powerfully with the personality of the person we will be considering. 'Bronstein's ego dominated his whole behavior', wrote an erstwhile comrade from Nikolaev days, A. G. Ziv, but 'the revolution dominated his ego', adding: 'He loved the workers and loved his comrades . . . because in them he loved his own self.' This seems consistent with the point made by Lunacharsky, who dismissed the charge of Trotsky being ambitious as 'utter nonsense', adding: 'There is not a drop of vanity in him, he is totally indifferent to any title or to the trappings of power; he is, however, boundlessly jealous of his own role in history, and in that sense he *is* ambitious.' An early functionary in the Communist International, Angelica Balabanoff, emphasized that 'more than any other figure in the Russian Revolution, Trotsky proved himself capable of arousing the masses by the force of his revolutionary temperament and his brilliant intellectual gifts.' Looking at the flip side, she commented: 'His arrogance equals his gifts and capacities and creates very often a distance between himself and those about him which excludes both personal warmth

With Trotsky in his Turkish and (in this photo) French exile were Rudolf Klement, Yvonne Crapeau, Jeanne Martin, Sara Jacob-Weber and a crouching Jean van Heijenoort.

and any feeling of equality and reciprocity.'[22] This may be too categorical – but is not entirely untrue.

Trotsky's first wife, Alexandra Sokolovskaya, was arrested with him in 1900, bearing two daughters in their Siberian internal exile. He had confessed to her that 'one can be more frank with the woman one loves than with oneself', but added that 'such frankness is possible only in personal conversation but not always, only in special and exceptional moments.' In 1902 he escaped from Siberia on his own, with her encouragement, to advance toward his rendezvous with history. Alexandra always remained supportive of her former husband's efforts and political perspectives, but had no difficulty in identifying his personal limitations. Trotsky could be very tender and sympathetic, she later commented, but was assertive and arrogant. She added that 'in all my experience I have never met any person so completely consecrated' to the revolutionary cause. In the 1930s she wrote to Trotsky, regarding his inability to help their troubled daughter Zinaida, that 'much is explained by your character, by the difficulty you have of expressing your feelings.' Lunacharsky more severely referred to Trotsky's 'unwillingness to show any human kindness or to be attentive to people; the absence of charm which always surrounded Lenin, condemned Trotsky to a certain loneliness.'[23]

This does not capture the entire reality. His second wife, Natalia Sedova, acknowledges that 'his circle of friends was small', mentioning from the 1917–28 period Christian Rakovsky, Nikolai Muralov, Ivan N. Smirnov, Yuri Pyatakov and Adolf Joffe, and she adds that he had 'cordial relations' with perhaps a dozen others. Part of Trotsky's tragedy was the loss of all of these relationships after 1929. There were very few – Alfred and Marguerite Rosmer from France, the exiled German revolutionaries Otto Rühle and Alice Rühle-Gerstel in Mexico – with whom he could share the intimacies of close friendship. 'Trotsky was very much at ease . . . without a trace of condescension but with the most delicate emphasis on absolute equality, combining extreme courtesy with complete informality', wrote Alice Rühle. 'He always behaves as if he were in our debt. So forthcoming, so warmly sympathetic, so friendly.'[24]

There were also, and always, the younger comrades. Natalia Sedova recalls that Trotsky 'established the warmest relationships' with comrades 'who were younger than himself and whom he hardly ever saw except at work', naming half a dozen secretaries and aides. One of Trotsky's secretaries during his years of exile, Sara Weber, corroborates: 'The youth, young comrades, were most precious to LD. Eagerly he would respond to their questions and often go over with them in personal conversation whatever points were raised.' She adds that 'there was never any "talking down" in LD – we were comrades, equals; there was simplicity

Trotsky in 1921.

and patience, and even the least knowledgeable could not feel slighted.' Describing his engagement with working-class militants who came to talk with him, Weber writes, 'I saw LD's attitude to working people; he knew and felt their lot. And for those attracted to revolutionary ideas, he never lacked the time; for them he had all the patience and tolerance and understanding.' At the same time, Weber could hardly avoid seeing another side of Trotsky when sharp differences arose within the Left Opposition of France. 'I felt the sweeping fury of LD's wrath . . . his words cutting, his eyes flashing blue sparks of fire – I saw before me the figure of Moses, breaking the tablets with the Ten Commandments . . . and felt shaken.'[25]

On the other hand, Weber recalls:

Half jokingly, and yet in deep earnest, LD would often say to young comrades: 'Do not listen to the old monkeys', meaning do not revere authority, do things on your own. 'Do not listen to the old monkeys', making no exception of himself. Natalia did not seem to accept that . . . LD was 53 years old at the time, energetic, young looking and handsome.[26]

The historical grandeur of the man must not be minimized. It comes through in the account of a 1917 mass meeting of more than 3,000 people in St Petersburg on the eve of the Bolshevik Revolution. Nikolai N. Sukhanov, a Menshevik opponent of the Bolsheviks that Trotsky had recently joined, describes what happened when Trotsky took the speakers' platform.

The Soviet regime was not only called upon to put an end to the suffering of the trenches. It would give land and heal the internal disorder. Once again the recipes against hunger were repeated: a soldier, a sailor, and a working girl, who would requisition bread from those who had it and distribute it free to the cities and front.

But Trotsky went even further on this decisive 'day of the St Petersburg Soviet.'

'The Soviet Government will give everything the country contains to the poor and the men in the trenches. You, bourgeois, have got two fur caps! – give one of them to the soldier, who's freezing in the trenches. Have you got warm boots? Stay at home. The worker needs your boots . . .'

These were very good and just ideas. They could not but excite the enthusiasm of a crowd who had been reared on the Tsarist whip. In any case, I certify as a direct witness that this was what was said on this last day.[27]

The mood of the crowd was 'bordering on ecstasy', Sukhanov recalled, and Trotsky formulated a brief resolution with words like 'we will defend the worker-peasant cause to the last drop of our blood'. And then the question was posed: Who was – *for*? According to Sukhanov, 'the crowd of thousands, as one man, raised their hands. I saw the raised hands and burning eyes of men, women, youths, soldiers, peasants, and – typically lower-middle-class faces.' As Trotsky continued, 'the innumerable crowd went on holding their hands up', and his words sealed their response into a sacred commitment: 'Let this vote of yours be your vow – with all your strength and at any sacrifice to support the Soviet that has taken on itself the glorious burden of bringing to a conclusion the victory of the revolution and of giving land, bread, and peace!'

Drawing from a quite different medium of expression, Trotsky's diary for 1935, the knowledgeable psychoanalyst Erich Fromm suggests a quite different dimension of the man:

No doubt Trotsky as an individual was as different from Marx, Engels and Lenin as they were among themselves; and yet in being permitted to have an intimate glimpse of the personal life of Trotsky, one is struck by all that he has in common with these productive personalities. Whether he writes about political events, or Emma Goldman's autobiography, or Wallace's detective stories, his reaction goes to the roots, is penetrating, alive and productive . . . In the midst of insecure exile, illness, cruel Stalinist persecution of his family, there is never a note of self-pity or even despair. There is objectivity and courage and humility. This is a modest man; proud of his cause, proud of the truth he discovers, but not vain or self-centered.[28]

The psychoanalyst might have dealt, also, with Trotsky's compulsions and breakdowns. 'He lived under great pressure, dealing with twenty different matters at once, reading documents, studying, and writing articles on literature, economics and domestic or foreign affairs', his companion Natalia Sedova later recounted. 'No wonder that his health began to suffer.' There were periodic debilitating illnesses: 'Apparently the constant conflict between Leon Davidovich's fine sensibility, nervous temperament and indomitable will brought on these attacks at moments of excessive mental strain.'[29]

This is the person, with all his brilliance and contradictions, to whom we will be giving our attention in this book.

1

The Shock of Exile

'Comrades, look! They're carrying off Comrade Trotsky!' As he shouted in defence of his father, young Lyova hammered on the doors of surrounding apartments in the building that contained his own home. It was 17 January 1928, and behind the closed doors were prominent members of the Russian Communist Party, who were by no means prepared to respond to these appeals by twenty-one-year-old Lev Sedov. Once second only to Lenin in the Communist pantheon, Trotsky was being carried away by the ominous 'they' – the GPU. The father was leader of the Left Opposition, and Lyova an energetic member of its youth wing. Lyova's nineteen-year-old younger brother, Sergei, who was relatively unpolitical in this intensely revolutionary family, nonetheless joined his brother in attempting to rally support, punching one GPU agent who clapped a hand over Lyova's mouth. The officer in charge, ashamed because he had served under Trotsky during the Civil War, lamented: 'Shoot me, Comrade Trotsky!' To which Trotsky responded: 'Don't talk nonsense, Kishkin. No one is going to shoot you. Go ahead with your job.' Yet the revolutionary chose not to cooperate with the arrest, forcing the GPU agents to break down the door and physically carry him away.[1]

The initials GPU (gay-pay-oo) stood for the Russian words *gosudarstvennoye politicheskoye upravlenie* – the State Political Directorate, which had succeeded the All-Russia Extraordinary Commission to Combat Counter-revolution and Sabotage – the infamous Cheka.[2] This had been created in 1918, through the initiation of Lenin himself and under the leadership of Felix Dzerzhinsky, to battle the thick networks of internal enemies seeking to bring down the young Soviet Republic. The Red Army, built up into a mighty force under Trotsky's leadership, did the same on the battlefields of the Russian Civil War. Dzerzhinsky, a seasoned Polish revolutionary and follower of Rosa Luxemburg, had gone over to the Bolsheviks in 1917, and by reputation was reliable, highly organized, incorruptible – and ruthless. He oversaw the Cheka's transformation into the GPU.[3] Fiercely opposed to the disunity he felt Trotsky's oppositional activities were generating within the revolutionary vanguard, he died of a heart attack in 1926 after denouncing such things at a Party meeting. Three years later, the repressive wheels of the Soviet state continued to grind forward as the GPU arrested Trotsky and took him away. Yet knowledgeable researchers would later comment that Dzerzhinsky's death 'came at a convenient time for Joseph Stalin', since he 'would almost certainly have resisted' the use of the GPU 'against dissent within the Party'. And he detested the bureaucratic leviathan arising in the Soviet Union: 'When I look at our apparatus, at our system of organization, our incredible bureaucracy and our utter disorder, cluttered with every sort of red tape, I am literally horrified.'[4]

Communist Authoritarianism

Rewinding Trotsky's life to the time when he was at the pinnacle of power, we see the organizer and commander of the Red Army, as multiple armies of internal and foreign enemies were engaging in a merciless war to bring down the just-born Soviet republic. The Russian army had disintegrated amidst war and revolution. How could the relatively rag-tag military forces available to the Soviet regime prevent the impending counter-revolutionary massacres?

A dozen major figures of the Communist regime in 1920: the upper arc shows Alexei Rykov, Karl Radek, Mikhail Pokrovsky and Lev Kamenev; in the middle are Trotsky, Lenin and Yakob Sverdlov; in the lower arc are Nikolai Bukharin, Gregory Zinoviev, Nikolai Krylenko, Alexandra Kollontai and Anatoly Lunacharsky.

'The front ranks of the masses had to realize the mortal danger of the situation', Trotsky later explained. 'The first requisite for success was to hide nothing, our weakness least of all; not to trifle with the masses but to call everything by its right name.' In his history of the Russian Civil War, historian W. Bruce Lincoln described 'the revolutionary orator of unmatched brilliance, whose fiery words inspired men and women to face great danger and perform greater feats in the name of the Revolution', adding that Trotsky 'sent men and women to Petrograd's defenses with their hearts seared by his revolutionary passion and comforted by his abiding belief in the new world the Bolsheviks were building'.[5]

Yet the ferocious enemies in the Civil War could hardly be defeated simply by oratory. Trotsky 'brought discipline to the shattered Bolshevik forces', Lincoln tells us, and Geoffrey Swain adds that 'the growth of the Red Army was astounding', rising from 372,000 to 475,000 during December 1918, and to 1,500,000 by mid-1919. There was the pitiless use of the death penalty as well: 'I give warning that if any unit retreats without orders, the first to be shot down will be the commissar [Communist political director] of the unit, and next the [military] commander.' Sometimes others would be made examples of as well. As long as there are wars, he later explained, 'the command will be obliged to place soldiers between the possible death at the front and the inevitable one in the rear.' Yet he insisted that 'the strongest cement of the new army was the ideas of the October Revolution.' It was a combination of factors that made the Red Army the formidable force that it became: propaganda, organization, revolutionary example and repression produced the necessary change through which 'heterogeneous detachments became regular units buttressed by worker-communists from Petrograd, Moscow and other places. The regiments stiffened up.' And they brought victory.[6]

In his angry polemics against the strictures of those who criticized Bolshevik brutality (such as Karl Kautsky, once considered 'the pope of Marxism'), Trotsky lashed out: 'We were never concerned with the Kantian-priestly and vegetarian-Quaker prattle about the "sacredness of human life". We were revolutionaries in opposition, and have remained revolutionaries in power. To make the individual sacred we must destroy the social order which crucifies him. And this problem can only be solved by blood and iron.' He added:

What is the meaning of the principle of the sacredness of human life in practice, and in what does it differ from the commandment, 'Thou shalt not kill', Kautsky does not explain. When a murderer raises his knife over a child, may one kill the murderer to save the child? Will not thereby the principle of the 'sacredness of human life' be infringed? May one kill the murderer to save oneself? Is an insurrection of oppressed slaves against their masters permissible? Is it permissible to purchase one's freedom at the cost of the life of one's jailers? If human life in general is sacred and inviolable, we must deny ourselves not only the use of terror, not only war, but also revolution itself . . . As long as human labor power, and, consequently, life itself, remain articles of sale and purchase, of exploitation and robbery, the principle of the 'sacredness of human life' remains a shameful lie, uttered with the object of keeping the oppressed slaves in their chains.[7]

Trotsky came to be seen as one of the more ruthless leaders of the early Communist state, even off the battlefield. 'Under socialism there will be no compulsion', he acknowledged, since 'the principle of compulsion contradicts socialism', under which the labouring majority that now owned and controlled the economy 'shall be moved by the feeling of duty, the habit of working, the attractiveness of labor', and in fact, 'under socialism there will not exist the apparatus of compulsion itself, namely the State: for it will have melted away entirely into a producing and consuming commune.' However, 'the road to socialism lies through a period of the highest possible intensification of the principle of the State', involving civil war and the struggles against the onslaughts of imperialism. 'Just as a lamp, before going out, shoots up in a brilliant flame, so the State, before disappearing, assumes the form of the dictatorship of the proletariat, i.e., the most ruthless form of State, which embraces the life of the citizens authoritatively in every direction.'[8]

True to Marxism's democratic core, Rosa Luxemburg had admonished: 'Socialist democracy does not come as some sort of Christmas present for the worthy people who, in the interim, have loyally supported a handful of socialist dictators.' But in these years of desperate violence, as the young Soviet Republic was viciously attacked and fighting for its life, Trotsky particularly, as the supreme commander of the Red Army, developed a style that

A modernistic illustration by Yuri Annenkov shows Trotsky as an imperious commander.

even Lenin – quite capable of pitiless authoritarian rhetoric – concluded was excessively 'administrative'. This put him at loggerheads with some of the working-class currents that had been drawn to his revolutionary eloquence in 1917. 'Under the form of the "struggle against despotic centralism" and against "stifling" discipline, a fight takes place for the self-preservation of various groups and subgroupings of the working class, with their petty ward leaders and their local oracles', he wrote in this period.

> The entire working class, while preserving its cultural originality and its political nuances, can act methodically and firmly without remaining in the tow of events and directing each time its mortal blows against the weak sectors of its enemies, on the condition that at its head, above the wards, the districts, the groups, there is an apparatus which is centralized and bound together by an iron discipline.[9]

In fact the bulk of the Bolshevik leadership, Lenin included, found itself in conflict with emerging currents of disappointed rank-and-file comrades, joined and mobilized by prominent Party dissidents in the early 1920s. One Communist militant remembered of the revolutionary years: 'We all lived in a state of revolutionary romanticism: weary and exhausted but happy, festive; unkempt, unwashed, long-haired and unshaven, but clear and clean of thought and heart.' A Communist returning from the Civil War wrote to Lenin that 'in the heart of every conscious comrade from the front, who at the front has become used to almost complete equality, who has broken from every kind of servility, debauchery and luxury – with which our very best party comrades now surround themselves – there boils hatred and disbelief.' A disillusioned party member explained in a letter of resignation: 'I cannot be that sort of idealist communist who believes in the new God That They Call the State, bows down before the bureaucracy that is so far from the working people, and waits for communism from the hands of pen-pushers and officials as though it was the kingdom of heaven.' In 1920 a leader of the Democratic Centralist faction in the Communist Party snapped: 'Why talk about the proletarian dictatorship or workers' self-activity? There's no self-activity here!' A manifesto of 1923 from the dissident Workers Group asserted:

> What are we being told? 'You sit quietly, go out and demonstrate when you're invited, sing the Internationale – when required – and the rest will be done without you, by first-class people who are almost the same sort of workers as you, only cleverer.' . . . But what we need is a practice based on the self-activity of the working class, not on the party's fear of it.[10]

Among the early working-class oppositional groups in and around the Russian Communist Party, the best known is the current led by Alexander Shlyapnikov and Alexandra Kollontai. Points made in their grouping's pamphlet, *The Workers Opposition*, resonated among many working-class militants:

> The workers may cherish an ardent affection and love for such personalities as Lenin. They may be fascinated by the incomparable flowery eloquence of Trotsky and his organizing abilities. They may revere a number of other leaders as leaders. But when the masses feel that they and their class are not trusted, it is quite natural that they say: 'No, halt! We refuse to follow you blindly . . .'
> The leaders are one thing, and we are altogether something different. Maybe it is true that the leaders know how to rule over the country, but they fail to understand our needs, our life in the shops, its requirements and immediate needs; they do not understand and do not know. From this reasoning follows the instinctive leaning towards the unions and dropping out of the party. 'It is true they are part of us, but as soon as they get into the centers, they leave us altogether; they begin to live differently. If we suffer, what do they care? Our sorrows are not theirs any longer.'[11]

The beliefs, sentiments and values underlying such deepening protest and dissent were at the heart of the profound ideal of workers' democracy, the very concept of socialism, the revolutionary Marxism animating the writings, speeches and activism that the Bolshevik Revolution of 1917 claimed to represent. While Lenin and Trotsky never renounced their earlier commitments, they insisted on the necessity of emergency measures – often given, as we see from Trotsky's comments, a sweepingly 'revolutionary' rationale. The reasons flowed more from reality than ideology, given the devastations of a brutalizing civil war, foreign military interventions and economic blockades, as well as inexperience in economic enterprise and governance, genuine plots and assassination attempts (some successful), not to mention the pre-Revolutionary calamities wrought by the First World War. In the name of defending the Revolution, a terrible violence was justified, which included the brutal repression of peasants who were simply defending their crops from confiscation, and of the angry sailors and workers who revolted at the Kronstadt naval base outside Petrograd, traditionally a centre of pro-Bolshevik strength.[12]

Lenin was more alert to what was going wrong than Trotsky. The Red Army commander had developed schemes for 'the militarization of labour' which included making trade unions instruments of the Soviet state. If the economy was under state control, and if this was a workers' state, then why would workers need to defend themselves or go on strike against their own government? Lenin helped to defeat Trotsky's sweeping proposals. Given the realities, workers actually needed protection from the regime. 'A workers' state is an abstraction', he insisted. 'What we actually have is a workers' state with this peculiarity, firstly, that it is not the working class but the peasant population that predominates in the country, and, secondly, that it is a workers' state with bureaucratic distortions.'[13]

As it turned out, these bureaucratic distortions were increasingly becoming the defining characteristic of the Soviet state – as the once-democratic councils became dominated exclusively by the Communist Party, and the Party became increasingly dominated by its administrative apparatus. The apparatus, in turn, came under the control of the newly created position of General Secretary – a powerful position combining the functions of clerk, coordinator of leadership meetings and personnel manager. Strategically placed at the intersection of the Communist Party and the Soviet state, the General Secretary would potentially be incredibly powerful, as the combined party-state bureaucracies assumed more and more control over the political, economic and cultural life of the Soviet Republic. The position was held by Joseph Stalin, a seasoned Bolshevik who was considered modest, efficient and reliable by many prominent comrades, but who had certain personal characteristics that were not fully understood.

Lenin himself began to look for ways to overcome the growing bureaucratic danger and to place workers and their peasant allies at the centre of state power, as they had been – all too fleetingly – in 1917. This effort itself became bureaucratized. Alarmed by the drift of events, Lenin came to feel that many prominent comrades were increasingly becoming part of the problem rather than part of the solution. This was especially the case thanks to policies initiated in 1921 as part of the New Economic Policy (NEP), which reinstituted aspects of capitalism in order to rebuild and revitalize the shattered economy. The increasing prosperity that resulted, creating more of an economic surplus, improved the quality of life for many, but created the possibility that greater material privileges would go to elements in the state and party apparatuses. Growing inequalities began to develop, despite the official rhetoric in favour of social equality. An even greater gulf began to develop between all those 'good Communists' at the top (who often developed arrogant conceits about their own wisdom, virtues

Stalin, 1927.

and capacities) and the masses of labouring people who created the growing economic surplus. The impact on political and economic policies was increasingly troubling. Lenin – undermined by a series of strokes that would soon end his life – began to form an anti-bureaucratic alliance with Trotsky, whose thinking was shifting along similar lines.[14]

One of the great tragedies of Bolshevism was that Lenin, Trotsky and other leaders had by 1922 crushed oppositional currents – the Workers' Opposition, Democratic Centralists and others – whose perspectives had been rooted deeply in Bolshevik ideals that culminated in the 1917 triumph. These currents had initially enjoyed significant support, but they were not allowed the space to challenge the ominous bureaucratization of which Lenin and Trotsky had now become keenly aware. Yet it was by no means clear that all was lost, despite the incapacitation and finally the death of Lenin.

Among many worker-Bolsheviks and pro-Bolshevik workers not inclined to engage in oppositional activity, there developed a profound sense of alienation. One worker swept up in the 1930s purges, befriended by the Communist Joseph Berger in the prison camps, explained why he and many workmates had avoided participation in any of the oppositions of the 1920s:

> We would have joined anyone – Shlyapnikov [of the Workers Opposition] or Sapronov [of the Democratic Centralists] or Trotsky himself – if we had thought it would do any good. What we thought was needed was a shift in power or at least a change of attitude towards the workers. But whichever group won, it would only mean a change at the top. And there was something else. It seemed to us that already then, and especially after Lenin's death, it was too late. They were doomed to fail because a new order was already established. The Party was no longer the Party we had known. We no longer had its confidence. But the last thing we could do was to stop trusting it. It was our whole life. It was still the Party . . . It was what we believed in . . . We *were* the Party and the State, and yet the State and the Party were somehow outside us. They were our religion, but they were no longer ourselves.[15]

'There is no doubt that Lenin suffered his greatest defeat when, with the outbreak of the civil war, the supreme power that he originally planned to concentrate in the Soviets definitely passed into the hands of the party bureaucracy', Hannah Arendt has noted in her classic study *The Origins of Totalitarianism*, perceptively emphasizing a point often overlooked in later years:

> At the moment of Lenin's death, the roads were still open. The formation of workers, peasants, and middle classes need not necessarily have led to class struggle which had been characteristic of European capitalism. Agriculture could still be developed on a collective, cooperative, or private basis, and the national economy was still free to follow a socialist, state-capitalist, or a free-enterprise pattern. None of these alternatives would have automatically destroyed the new structure of the country.[16]

This moment of openness – facilitated by the economic recovery associated with the New Economic Policy – was noted and discussed by a variety of perceptive and articulate observers, as well as latter-day scholars.[17] But positive outcomes could hardly be expected to emerge from the accelerating bureaucratic drift.

The Shift to Opposition

We have seen that it was Lenin who had drawn Trotsky into an effort to push against bureaucracy – a partnership extending from the latter portion of 1922 to early 1923, after which Lenin was no longer able to function. Isaac Deutscher tells us that 'in the first half of 1922 Trotsky still spoke primarily as the Bolshevik disciplinarian; in the second half he was already in conflict with the disciplinarians', coming 'closer to the Workers Opposition and kindred groups' –

Trotsky and his
son Lyova in the
early 1920s.

not accepting what he believed to be utopian, unrealistic aspects
of their positions, but 'acknowledging the rational side of their
revulsion against authority . . . He began to protest against the
excesses of centralism as these made themselves felt . . . He clashed
with the party "apparatus" as the apparatus grew independent
of the party and subjected party and state to itself.' Deutscher
emphasizes a growing cleavage between 'the power and the dream'
– and the deepening contradiction felt by the Bolsheviks who had
created a machine of power to make the dream a reality. 'They
could not dispense with power if they were to strive for the
fulfillment of their ideals; but now their power came to oppress
and overshadow their ideals.' Deutscher added: 'Nobody had in
1920–1 gone farther than Trotsky in demanding that every interest
and aspiration should be wholly subordinated to the "iron

dictatorship." Yet he was the first of the Bolshevik chiefs to turn against the machine of that dictatorship when it began to devour the dream.'[18]

Seen by most of the world as second only to Lenin in authority among the Bolsheviks, Trotsky was actually a latecomer. Of course, since his late teens he had been committed, heart, body, mind and soul, to the cause of revolutionary socialism. Close to Lenin up to the 1903 Second Congress of the Russian Social Democratic Labour Party (RSDLP), he broke away, along with the Menshevik faction, over Lenin's insistence on a disciplined and centralized party. In his 1904 polemic *Our Political Tasks*, Trotsky challenged Lenin's orientation with the following argument (similar, as we can see, to the complaints of dissident Communists in the early 1920s):

> In the one case we have a party which *thinks for* the proletariat, which *substitutes itself* politically for it, and in the other we have a party which politically *educates* and *mobilizes* the proletariat to exercise rational pressure on the will of all political groups and parties . . . In the internal politics of the Party these methods [of Lenin] lead . . . to the Party organization 'substituting' itself for the Party, the Central Committee substituting itself for the Party organization, and finally the dictator substituting himself for the Central Committee; on the other hand, this leads the committees to supply an 'orientation' – and to change it – while 'the people keep silent.'[19]

Trotsky concluded, in 1917, that Lenin's organizational views were correct, but he also seems to have felt that he had distorted Lenin's position, which (he was confident) stood much closer to his own. Indeed, Lenin insisted in November 1917 that 'there has been no better Bolshevik' than Trotsky.

An essential quality of Trotsky's revolutionary character was a commitment *not to lie*, not to compromise the truth for the purpose of advancing one's own position, or even of getting along with comrades, but instead to insist on truth. This permeated his own conception of what it meant to be a good Bolshevik. 'A Bolshevik is not merely a disciplined person; he is a person who in each case and on each question forges a firm opinion of his own and defends it courageously and independently, not only against his enemies but inside his own party. Today, perhaps, he will be in the minority in his organization. He will submit, because it is his party. But this does not always signify that he is in the wrong.' And if he is right, by persistently raising his differences, 'he will render his party a service.' What the party needs is not 'sycophantic functionaries' but people 'who are strongly tempered morally, permeated with a feeling of personal responsibility'. He emphasized: 'What is needed is criticism, checking of fact, independence of thought, independence of character, the feeling of responsibility, truth toward oneself and toward one's work.'[20]

The just-quoted passages come from Trotsky's articles of 1923 entitled *The New Course*, part of a general upwelling within the Russian Communist Party expressing a dissatisfaction over the slow rate of industrialization, the deterioration of working-class living and working conditions, the growth of bureaucracy and the lack of genuine inner-party democracy. This mood was expressed in factories, in educational institutions, even within the military. In each sector representatives of the central Communist Party leadership found themselves sharply challenged, with sentiments visibly shifting in the direction of a loosely organized Left Opposition associated with Trotsky. (In fact, the Left Opposition had to be quite 'loose' since organized oppositional groups had been outlawed in the Communist Party after a 1921 ban on factions.) Among the comrades associated with him were Christian Rakovsky, Adolf Joffe, Karl Radek, Evgeny Preobrazhensky, Ivan Smilga, Vladimir Antonov-Ovseenko, Gregory Pyatakov, Ivan Smirnov – heroes of the Revolution and Civil War, some with quite substantial Bolshevik credentials stretching back for years before 1917, all with highly responsible positions in the Soviet government.[21]

Within the central leadership of the Russian Communist Party at this time, there had formed a 'troika' consisting of the General Secretary, Stalin, and two of Lenin's most prominent lieutenants, Gregory Zinoviev (head of the Communist Party in Leningrad and chairman of the Communist International), and Lev Kamenev (head of the Communist Party in Moscow and editor of the party newspaper *Pravda*). As Trotsky noted in the historical essay 'Lessons of October', also published in 1923, Lenin had broken with these two lieutenants over whether the Bolsheviks should actually move forward to revolution in October/November 1917 – a step they fiercely opposed (in contrast to Lenin, Trotsky and the Bolshevik majority). There had been a speedy reconciliation, but the two had become closely aligned with Stalin, helping to blunt the impact of Lenin's criticism of the tyrant-in-waiting whom they, like many, still greatly underestimated.

Left Oppositionists – back, from left: Christian Rakovsky, Yakov Drobnis, Alexander Beloborodov, Lev Sosnovsky; front: Leonid Serebriakov, Karl Radek, Trotsky, Mikhail Boguslovsky and Evgeni Preobrazhensky.

The person they really distrusted was the brilliant and charismatic newcomer Trotsky. The troika systematically lined up some of the prominent Old Bolsheviks as well as the Party apparatus around a campaign against 'Trotskyism' (a fabrication that Zinoviev and Kamenev concocted to intimidate and discredit the Left Opposition, as they later apologetically admitted to Trotsky himself). Much was made of Trotsky's well-known formulation of the theory of permanent revolution, which was denounced as anti-Leninist. In a symposium on *The Errors of Trotskyism*, even Lenin's widow, Nadezhda Krupskaya, was enlisted to challenge Trotsky, although she could not help but soften her own critique: 'Comrade Trotsky devoted the whole of his powers to the fight for the Soviet power during the decisive years of the revolution. He held out heroically in his difficult and responsible position. He worked with unexampled energy and accomplished wonders in the interests of the safeguarding of the victory of the revolution. The Party will not forget this.' Zinoviev was more severe: 'To replace Leninism by Trotskyism, that is the task which Comrade Trotsky has set out to accomplish.' And Stalin even more so: 'The duty of the Party is to bury Trotskyism as a line of thought.' A joint plenum of the Russian Communist Party's leadership bodies declared: 'Comrade Trotsky is again raising the question of the fundamental alteration of the leadership of the Party and is advocating views which have been categorically condemned by that Congress, the plenum of the Central Committee and the Central Control Committee.'[22]

In the face of this onslaught, Trotsky urged his supporters to pull back. More than this, the immense pressures caused Trotsky to play false with his own beliefs. He renounced his theory of permanent revolution. He denounced as 'a tool of counter-revolution' a book containing the first public revelation of Lenin's testament, *Since Lenin Died* by the u.s. radical journalist Max Eastman, with whom Trotsky had been close. And he asserted at the Thirteenth Party

Congress of 1925: 'Comrades, none of us wishes to be right against the party. In the last instance the party is always right, because it is the only historic instrument which the working class possesses for the solution of its fundamental tasks.' It is interesting to note the role of Lenin's widow at this time. According to her biographer Robert H. McNeal, it was actually Krupskaya who had been behind the surreptitious delivery of Lenin's testament to Max Eastman (who had first heard of it, however, from Trotsky). And at the Thirteenth Congress she openly rejected the notion that the Party is infallible, in a later intervention insisting: 'One cannot soothe one's self with the thought that the majority is always right. In the history of the party there have been times when the majority was not right.' Moreover she was indignant over demands for Trotsky to recant presumably heretical views, calling this 'psychologically impossible', claiming that it would introduce 'superfluous bitterness' into the functioning of the Party, cutting across its capacity to cope thoughtfully with current problems. 'And this obligation is stronger than ever because Vladimir Ilyich is not with us.' (Trotsky would reflect in his diary of 1935 that Krupskaya had 'consistently and firmly refused to act against her conscience'.)[23]

United Opposition: Struggle and Defeat

Recovering his balance, Trotsky would soon renew and deepen his opposition, and in future years – regardless of almost unbearable pressures and inevitable errors – would never cease to be true to himself. Indeed, within 24 months Trotsky and his co-thinkers would join together with a much more substantial layer within the Party – including Zinoviev, Kamenev and Krupskaya – to form the United Opposition in 1926–7.

In their initial 'Declaration of the Thirteen', Kamenev, Krupskaya, Trotsky, Zinoviev and other prominent comrades laid out a comprehensive critique of the recomposed leadership team gathered around Stalin and Nikolai Bukharin. Key points of the declaration deal with an overly conservative agricultural policy favouring well-to-do peasants, and go-slow industrialization policies linked to sagging wage rates for the workers. No less substantial was the challenge to the notion advanced by Stalin that it would be possible to build socialism in a single country – the Soviet Union. 'All dubious theoretical innovations must be thrown out if they portray matters as though the victory of socialist construction in our country were not inseparably connected with the progress and outcome of the struggle for power by the European and world proletariat', the declaration insisted. 'The colonial peoples are fighting for independence. We are all fighting on the same front. Each unit at each sector of the front must do the maximum within its power without waiting for the initiatives of the others.' The conclusion stresses: 'Socialism will be victorious in our country in inseparable connection with the revolutions of the European and world proletariat and with the struggle of the East against the imperialist yoke.'[24]

The *socialism in one country* perspective caused – for all practical purposes – a downgrade in the seriousness with which the Communist International was taken. Initially established by Lenin and his comrades to build parties in countries throughout the world, based on the perceived link between the possibility of building socialism in backward Russia and the triumph of socialist revolutions elsewhere, the Communist International was now being transformed into a tool of Soviet foreign policy as alliances were sought with powerful, but not necessarily revolutionary elements throughout the world. What the historian E. H. Carr referred to as the change in aim and direction 'from active promotion of world revolution to the use of foreign communist parties as the spearheads of more cautious policies favored in Moscow' was obligatory for the Communist Party leaderships of various countries (if they wished to remain in the Communist movement). Strong ties were developed, for example, with reformist trade union bureaucrats in Britain who participated in an Anglo-Russian Committee (dedicated to solidarity between British and Soviet workers), who were happy to buttress their own radical credentials but who, nonetheless, were quite prepared to sell out the British General Strike of 1926. Even more disastrous was the Comintern's close ties with Chinese Nationalist Party leader Generalissimo Chiang Kai-shek, who maintained a superficial friendship with the USSR and worked with the Chinese Communists to reunify the country by defeating warlord fragmentation. In 1927, however, he murderously turned against the substantial Communist movement in China, driving its shattered remnants deep into the countryside.[25]

Running through the entire document even more powerfully, however, was an insistence on the dangers posed by bureaucratic dictatorship and the necessity of working-class democracy:

> The immediate cause of the increasingly severe crises in the party is bureaucratism, which has grown appallingly in the period since Lenin's death and continues to grow . . . It is quite clear that it is more and more difficult for the leadership to carry out its policies by methods of party democracy, the less the vanguard of the working class perceives these policies as its own. The divergence in direction between economic policies and the thoughts and feelings of the proletarian vanguard inevitably strengthens the need for high-pressure methods and imparts an administrative-bureaucratic character to all politics . . . How many times Lenin referred to the bureaucratic deformations in the state apparatus and to the need for the trade unions, on frequent occasions, to defend the workers from the Soviet state. But it is precisely in this area that the party bureaucrat is infected with delusions and self-deception

of the most dangerous kind . . . Bureaucratism strikes heavily at the worker in all spheres – in the party, economy, domestic life, and culture . . . The question of excesses of those on top is totally bound up with the suppression of criticism. The deepgoing dissatisfaction with the party regime established after Lenin's death, and the still greater dissatisfaction over the shifts in policy, inevitably produce oppositional outbursts and give rise to heated disputes. But the leading group, instead of learning from the new and ever more striking facts that appear, and instead of rectifying its political line, systematically deepens the errors of bureaucratism . . . Only on the basis of party democracy is healthy collective leadership possible. There is no other way.[26]

Part of the significance of this United Opposition is that it was *not* 'Trotskyist' – the majority of its leadership was made up of seasoned veterans of Bolshevism, Lenin's comrades for many years before 1917, who had held responsible positions in the revolutionary movement and the Soviet regime. Trotsky was by no means the leader here – he was a prominent part of a collective force that was reaching out to rank-and-file Communists and to as much of the Soviet working class as possible. As a concession to Zinoviev and Kamenev, he was still dismissive of his theory of permanent revolution – but the 'Declaration of the Thirteen', embraced by some of Lenin's most venerable associates, would constitute the core of what would be identified as 'Trotskyism' decades later.

Out of 750,000 Communist Party members, however, not more than 8,000 were in the United Opposition (perhaps evenly split among those led by Trotsky and those led by Zinoviev), so the obvious task was to win more of the Party to their orientation. Previously top-level Bolsheviks would now visit factory workers in their modest apartments, 'where up to fifty of them would cram together after work', recalled participant Victor Serge.

Trotsky, Lev Kamenev and Gregory Zinoviev surrounded by others in the United Opposition.

'A long time before, Party leaders had given up all direct contact with the masses, who knew them only from their portraits but now received them with the utmost warmth. The most difficult problems were frankly discussed in a friendly atmosphere while students kept watch outside.'

Secrecy was dictated by the decision of the authorities to persecute dissidents. 'Similar meetings were held in garages, woods and even in cemeteries as if the Party was beginning to come out of a long winter's sleep.' Trotsky later recalled: 'In one day I would visit two, three, and sometimes four such meetings.' Participants varied – 20, 100, 200, he noted, adding that about 20,000 attended such meetings in Leningrad (the new name for Petrograd) and in Moscow. Estimated membership in the Opposition rose to 10,000, with an additional layer of sympathizers twice that number.[27]

Such efforts brought escalating violence from Party-majority gangs of thugs, and an agreement was reached between the

Opposition and the Stalin-Bukharin leaders that Oppositional speakers would present their views only at official Party meetings. The meetings were packed, with organized squads of hecklers who often interrupted and even shouted down the speakers. Even those who had once viewed the Opposition leaders as genuine revolutionary heroes knew, if they were Communist Party members, that there would be no future for them if they were swayed by the Opposition. Joseph Freeman, a thoughtful u.s. Communist who listened to one of the final debates at a gathering of the Communist International, and was determined to maintain his own position in the movement, focused more on physical characteristics than the arguments, seeing 'Zinoviev plump with self-assurance, well fed on authority' and 'Kamenev, following Zinoviev, [who] looked like a mild little professor lecturing on paleontology' – although he acknowledged that he was 'a subtle debater who made important accusations'. But it was the fallen Trotsky that people most wanted to hear. 'Our eyes watched his body, compact and graceful. You felt at once how intensely personal he was.' Yet Freeman and others felt a need to steel themselves: 'The revolution disappeared before the man; his whole being demanded personal attention.' Nonetheless:

> This was what everyone had waited for, a brilliant drama with an attractive hero, a hero politically wrong, doomed to defeat, but greatly gifted and still regarded with the remains of a once boundless affection. The baritone poured out glamorous polemic. The ax of metaphor and invective fell mercilessly upon heads of foes.

Yet for Freeman, in the end, 'it was all magnificent rhetoric, and moral force, and intellectual brilliance, and all personal, as if the whole dispute were really nothing more than one over the relative merits of Trotsky and everyone else.' He concluded, self-protectively: 'This was perhaps the chief psychological limitation of the magnificent narcissist which frustrated his unusual talents' and forced him politically into 'a blind alley dank with counter-revolutionary spleen'.[28]

Stalin's erstwhile ally Kamenev warned Trotsky at one point: 'Do you think Stalin is now considering how to reply to your arguments? You are mistaken. He is thinking of how to destroy you.' Trotsky later reflected: 'Stalin was fighting to concentrate power in the hands of the bureaucracy and to expel the opposition from his ranks, while we were fighting for the interests of the international revolution and thus setting ourselves against the conservatism of the bureaucracy and its longing for tranquility, prosperity and comfort.' This bureaucracy was absolutely not going to tolerate any threat to the realization of such longings. Brutal and intensifying pressures were brought to bear, to which some oppositionists began to succumb. Krupskaya confided to Kamenev, 'If Lenin were alive today, he would be in jail.' Stalin is said to have threatened darkly to 'make someone else Lenin's widow', with degrading comments and crude, scandalous rumours about Krupskaya put into circulation within the Party and state apparatus and even among the Communist youth. Speculations about the danger of war with Western countries were brought into play, with the argument that now, more than ever, unity was needed in Communist ranks – and at this point Krupskaya broke from oppositional activity. (In later years she felt compelled to publicly support all Stalin's measures, including murderous ones which she detested.) Many others, not counting on the incredible repressions, did likewise.[29]

The historian Michal Reiman, combing through official Soviet documents, has reported: 'News of organizational measurers against the opposition and arrests of its supporters came from all major cities – Leningrad, Kiev, Tblisi, Yeveran, Rostov on the Don, and elsewhere', with an uptick of physical assaults on opposition meetings and oppositionists. 'Almost everywhere, oppositionists were fired and blacklisted, working-class members of the opposition being especially hit hard.'[30]

In November 1927 there were to be massive celebrations in Leningrad and Moscow for the tenth anniversary of the Bolshevik Revolution. Zinoviev, Kamenev, Trotsky and others decided that Oppositionists should participate with their own banners and slogans (perhaps speeches as well) calling for workers' democracy and an end to corruption and bureaucracy, carrying out Lenin's Testament. Alerted to what was planned, the central leadership of the Party 'mobilized not only the party apparatus but also the GPU, with all its resources, against the upcoming opposition demonstrations', according to Reiman. While Oppositionists found some expressions of surprised elation from the crowds, and some confused efforts to protect the Oppositionists, the predominant note was struck, as Reiman reports, by 'Stalinist goon squads ('fighting units') and groups organized by the GPU and party apparatus [that] broke up the opposition columns as they formed and provoked scuffles that developed into full-scale brawls.' Gangs tore up the 'unofficial' placards and banners and hooted down Opposition leaders, some of whom 'had difficulty escaping from the violence of the hired mob'. The message of Zinoviev in Leningrad to a sceptical Trotsky in Moscow exuded an incredible optimism: 'All the information at hand indicates this will greatly benefit our cause.' Presumably he was counting on a backlash in favour of the Opposition.[31]

Instead there was a rapid move to expulsions – with Trotsky, Zinoviev and Kamenev heading the list. Zinoviev was desperate to stay in the Party, where he hoped to still help influence events and await at least partial vindication. His scribbled note to Trotsky, as they faced a wrathful majority at the fifteenth Party Congress, said: 'Leon Davidovich, the hour has come when we should have the courage to capitulate.' Trotsky scribbled back: 'If that kind of courage were enough, the revolution would have been won all around the world by now.' Expulsions came down on both the recanting Zinoviev and the defiant Trotsky, who denounced Stalin as 'the gravedigger of the Revolution'. According to official statistics, 3,258 were expelled and 3,381 recanted.[32]

In protest against the expulsions, an ailing Adolf Joffe committed suicide, leaving behind an amazing and eloquent letter explaining his action, offering his own philosophy of life and death, admonishing Trotsky for having made too many recent compromises (including renouncing his theory of permanent revolution) and urging him to continue the principled struggle. It was an act of courage for 10,000 people to attend his funeral on 19 November 1927, and here Trotsky would make his last public speech on Soviet soil, concluding: 'Let us take our leave of him in the same spirit that he lived and fought; he took his stand under the banner of Marx and Lenin; under that banner he died. And we vow to you, Adolf Abramovich, we will carry your banner through to the end!'[33]

The GPU was now preparing to arrest thousands of Oppositionists and send them into internal exile in areas in and near Siberia. Packing his thousands of books and innumerable documents, manuscripts and correspondence, Trotsky continued to meet with comrades, friends, journalists and others. He explained to one journalist that the current Soviet regime was 'bringing in the counterrevolution', and he challenged the notion – put forward by former British prime minister David Lloyd George – that he aimed at the sort of military dictatorship that Napoleon Bonaparte had represented. Some believed he was foolish not to use his military influence to win the factional struggle, and even some of his Soviet supporters in the military urged him to carry out 'a limited military coup' to 'sweep away Stalin's clique and restore Party democracy', as historian Pierre Broué has put it. But Trotsky was too much the Marxist to put his faith in anything other than a revolutionary working class – a purely military coup was anathema to him. 'I am no Napoleon; Lloyd George is once again mistaken', scoffed the

Trotsky making his last public speech in the Soviet Republic, at the semi-legal mass gathering at the funeral of his close comrade Adolph A. Joffe, 19 November 1927.

former Red Army commander. To his fellow Oppositionist Victor Serge, he said: 'We have begun a fight to the finish which may last for years and require many sacrifices. I am leaving for Central Asia. You try and leave for Europe. Good luck!' Another frequent visitor was Alexandra Kollontai of the old Workers' Opposition, elements of which had joined in the recent oppositional struggle. Natalia Sedova recalled: 'When she was appointed Ambassador to Norway, she came to take her leave of us and offered to take out Opposition documents in her diplomatic bags to hand over to foreign [dissident-Communist] groups.' But something happened to change matters, for when Natalia came to her with the materials a few days later, the once-courageous Kollontai was 'completely changed, confused and absolutely terrified. "I really can't take anything, I am sorry," she kept repeating.'[34]

Exile

On 16 January 1928 Trotsky was scheduled to be transported by train to Alma-Ata, his place of exile. The GPU was to arrive at

10 p.m. to take Trotsky, his wife and whatever children would be accompanying them to the train station. Packed and ready to go, they waited for GPU agents who simply did not appear. Meanwhile, at the train station, thousands had gathered, shouting 'Long live Trotsky!' A huge portrait of Trotsky was set up on one of the train cars, to the cheering of the crowds. A contingent of workers blocked the train, and others vainly searched the train for Trotsky. There were clashes with the police and the GPU, with casualties on both sides and arrests. The departure was officially postponed for two days.[35] But the official date of postponement was a half-truth – the GPU showed up the following day, and the scene with which this chapter opened was played out.

Bundled into the GPU automobile, then reaching the almost empty station, where Lyova again vainly attempted to arouse support, the family separated. The relatively unpolitical younger son Sergei, a mathematician, chose to stay in Moscow to complete his studies. Lyova chose to accompany his parents. (Trotsky's daughters, who had also been active in the Opposition, along with his first wife Alexandra Solokovskaya in Leningrad, did not have a choice. In any event the two young women were starting families of their own.)

Travelling for days through the countryside, then wastelands and snowstorms, then changing from train to bus, Trotsky, Natalia and Lyova arrived finally at their new home in Alma-Ata. It was 'a town of earthquakes and floods at the foot of the Tyan-Shan range on the borders of China, two hundred and fifty kilometers from the railway and four thousand from Moscow', Natalia Sedova later wrote in her diary, 'a year spent with letters, books, and nature'. She later added: 'It was also a year of secret and precious tokens of sympathy and moral communion with a revolutionary elite, men possessed of truly exceptional human qualities.' They were able to rent a small house close to the centre of town. 'Leon Davidovich buried himself in a mass of newspapers and manuscripts that covered every table and

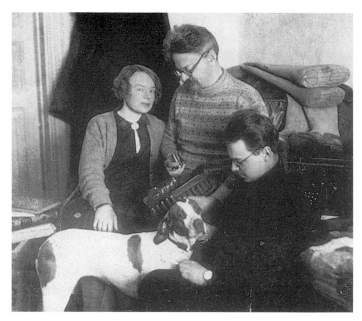

Trotsky, Natalia and Lyova exiled in Alma-Ata.

spilled over onto the rest of what sketchy furniture we had.' Since entering the Soviet government at the end of 1917, he had become used to dictating his writing to secretaries, and they were able to secure one in Alma-Ata, 'a charming young woman [who] had to make long reports about her work to the GPU', to take the extensive daily dictation that resulted in Trotsky's critique of the Bukharin-Stalin draft programme of the Communist International.

The critique later became *The Third International after Lenin*. Rooted in the programme of the United Opposition, it described the bureaucratic-conservative nature of the current Soviet regime, challenging the conception of building socialism in a single country: this represented a 'skinflint reactionary utopia of self-sufficient socialism' that had little to do with the actual socialist goal.[36] Genuine socialism could only be created on the basis of relative abundance, and as part of the transition from global capitalism to worldwide socialism. To this could be traced the decline of democracy in the Soviet Union, the intensifying authoritarianism of the Communist International and the proliferation of policies imposed on the parties of the International that were rooted in power struggles in the Soviet Union and in opportunistic foreign policy considerations that were detrimental to building genuinely revolutionary parties. Copies of Trotsky's critique somehow ended up in the packets of materials given to a small number of delegates at the Sixth Congress of the Communist International in 1928. The critique had a powerful impact on key leaders of the u.s. and Canadian Communist Parties, James P. Cannon and Maurice Spector, who would soon begin building the Left Opposition in North America.

From April to October Trotsky was able to maintain a lively correspondence, especially within the region of exile among fellow Oppositionists (about 8,000 had been arrested, with perhaps 2,000 'die-hards' sent into exile). Estimating that half of the correspondence did not get through, this still added up to about 800 political letters (some quite substantial) and 550 telegrams going out, and about 1,000 political letters and 700 telegrams coming in. Some of the correspondence involved growing disagreements among the Oppositionists. Some comrades had concluded that the counter-revolution was now complete, that the Soviet Union had now become some variant of state-capitalism and that a new revolution would be necessary – a position that Trotsky was absolutely not prepared to adopt. Other Oppositionists, wearying of exile's isolation, were hopeful over Stalin's break with Bukharin in order to initiate more rapid industrialization policies. They were beginning to suggest that capitulation (*à la* Zinoviev) might make sense – a position that Trotsky, insistent on the need for democratization, sharply rejected. One of the pieces of correspondence, not allowed through until it was too late, was intensely personal – a message

While in exile in 1911, Trotsky was visited by his older daughter Nina. She would succumb to tuberculosis while in her early 20s, at the start of Trotsky's second exile.

from his 26-year-old daughter Nina that she was dying of tuberculosis.[37]

By October Trotsky's correspondence was cut off altogether. When he protested, he was told it was in reaction to his 'counter-revolutionary' activity. Stalin and his closest associates in the Communist Party's Politburo had made the decision to expel him from the Soviet Union. This was done over the objection of Bukharin and his co-thinkers Soviet Premier Alexi Rykov and trade union leader Mikhail Tomsky – the so-called 'Right Opposition' whose commitment to more moderate policies on various matters was being assaulted and overwhelmed on one issue after another.[38]

Soon Trotsky, Natalia Sedova and Lev Sedov were transported on the steamship *Ilyich* to Turkey, arriving in Istanbul on 12 February 1929.

2

Revolutionary, Past and Present

The exile in Turkey was incredibly fruitful for 'the Pen'. The lifelong revolutionary activist was blocked from engaging directly in the swirling upsurges brought on by the global economic crisis of capitalism. Yet the enforced quiescence, and the relative freedom allowed him, enabled Trotsky to connect with innumerable activists, journalists, others – and above all to write. A powerful political intervention was achieved through volumes that came forth in this phase of his exile – as he put the finishing touches on the incisive polemic *Permanent Revolution* (begun in Alma-Ata), laboured over the rich memoir *My Life* and fashioned the three-volume classic *The History of the Russian Revolution*.

Trotsky arrived in one of the world's most ancient and amazing cities, whose succession of names – Byzantium, Constantinople, Istanbul – reflected a layered, wondrous, complex blend of Europe, the Middle East and Asia befitting a metropolis at the crossroads. Vibrantly intermingling ancient and modern cultures, it was undergoing new transformations under a forward-looking nationalist regime headed by Mustafa Kemal (with the titles of Pasha [Lord] and Atatürk [Father of the Turks]), president of the newly established Republic of Turkey. During the First World War the Ottoman Turks had been aligned with the losing side. When the war-shattered Ottoman Empire was preyed upon by victorious European powers in the wake of that defeat, Kemal – a nationalistic army officer – had led a successful war of independence. Feeling a natural affinity to Trotsky, he promised him freedom and security (watched over by vigilant but unobtrusive Turkish policemen) for as long as he lived in Turkey.

Trotsky's first weeks in Istanbul were spent in the Soviet Embassy, where an initial attitude of respect grew increasingly chilly. Despite Kemal's assurances, Trotsky and those around him were concerned about the large number of counter-revolutionary Russian exiles living in the city as well as the long arm of the GPU, and they secured a dilapidated two-storey house on the largest of the relatively secluded Princes' Islands (then Prinkipo, now Büyükada) in the Sea of Marmara, a short boat ride from Istanbul.

'The waves of the Sea of Marmara lapped the shore just a few steps from our new home', Natalia remembered. 'It was a beautiful place, spacious, peaceful, set in the blue sea and bathed in golden sunlight most of the time.' Sara Weber, one of many volunteers from various countries flocking to assist Trotsky, said of the house that 'a thicket of prickly shrubs protected it from the sea. LD's and Natalia's room just as LD's study were upstairs. Young comrades occupied downstairs rooms; in addition to their secretarial work, the "boys" stood guard night and day by turn.' English-language translator Max Eastman commented: 'He does not live in luxury; there is practically no furniture in his villa. It is a barrack, and the food is simple to the extreme.' Eastman's judgement was severe: 'The lack of comfort or beauty in Trotsky's house seems also despicable to me. A man and woman must be almost dead aesthetically to live in that bare barrack, which a very few dollars could convert into a charming house.'[1]

This was not Trotsky's purpose, however. In the early morning he and others would do some fishing or hunting to help replenish the food supply of the 'barrack'. According to Jean Van Heijenoort, a French comrade who served in the Trotsky household-in-exile for a number of years, after such exploits 'we would return to the house at eight to have a quick, simple breakfast of tea and goat

The villa on the island of Prinkipo which housed Trotsky, family members and aides.

cheese. Natalia prepared the tea and poured it for everybody.' Sara Weber tells us that at breakfast, Trotsky 'would rapidly butter the bread for Natalia, sitting alongside of him (he did everything rapidly) and, though his thoughts were engaged elsewhere, he would remain quietly attentive to her throughout the meal.' Immediately afterwards Trotsky and a secretary would go upstairs where he would walk back and forth, often until lunch, dictating 'in resonant tones' texts for correspondence, articles and pamphlets, and books. 'But for a brief after-lunch period, LD remained at his desk throughout the day and late into the evening.' Weber functioned as one of his secretaries and later recalled: 'Watching him dictate I had an almost *physical* sense of his thought processes; the thinking was so intense it seemed I could *feel* it. His thoughts were transformed into words, sentences, paragraphs, as if read from some inner memory tape.' Natalia recalled him commenting: 'It is as if the brain were working all by itself. The brain has its own momentum and all I have to do is to follow it . . .'.[2]

Trotsky's brain did not bring joy to all, at least on a personal level. Max Eastman, indignant over Trotsky's refusal to take him

Most of Trotsky's writings after 1917 were dictated – a habit continued up to his final exile in Mexico, as is shown here.

seriously, wrote: 'Trotsky is preoccupied with ideas and the world, but they are his own ideas and his own view of the world.' Eastman added that Trotsky's 'arrogance differs from vanity' because it was unconscious, and he shared the comments of Trotsky's first wife, Alexandra Sokolovskaya (whom he had once interviewed): 'Arrogance would be a better word than pride. Leon Davidovich is self-assertive and explosive, a little difficult that way sometimes in personal life, but he is the most consecrated person I ever met. Nothing, absolutely nothing – not even a disgraceful death – would swerve him from the path of his objective duty to the revolution.'[3] Trotsky's primary purpose, in his final exile, was to share as much as possible, as widely as possible, with actual and potential revolutionary activists before his mind blinked out of existence.

Connecting with Comrades

Trotsky devoted considerable energy to establishing and consolidating contacts with activists throughout the world, particularly among dissidents and oppositionists in the Communist movement, including inside the Soviet Union. For his entire sojourn in Turkey, he was convinced that the Soviet Union, while suffering from severe bureaucratic degeneration and a fatal lack of democracy, remained a workers' state worth fighting to reform. And although Communist Parties of all countries suffered from undemocratic debilitations, he favoured revolutionaries organizing not to create new parties, but to win the memberships of these already existing parties back to the original 'Bolshevik-Leninist' principles.

A primary concern was with helping strengthen oppositional currents inside the Communist Party of the Soviet Union. While the great majority of Left Oppositionists had been expelled and were languishing in internal exile, there remained a small network, operating in secret, with some base among industrial workers. Broader elements within the Party were increasingly critical of the leadership and policies of Stalin, including some who previously had fiercely opposed Trotsky. To connect with and influence such people, Trotsky and those who worked with him published the Russian-language *Bulletin of the Opposition*. Although its frequency was irregular, 65 separate issues appeared between 1929 and 1941, with a press run of about 1,000, ranging from 12 to 68 double-columned pages. Trotsky's analyses were published there, and articles by the *Bulletin*'s editor, Lev Sedov, as well as from prominent Communist dissidents of various countries. In the early 1930s knowledgeable underground activists in the USSR, and even quiet dissidents with positions of responsibility in the Soviet state and Communist Party, provided information and even wrote articles under pseudonyms for the *Bulletin*. 'Most senior officials and members of Soviet missions abroad made a point of reading the *Bulletin*, memorized its contents and some even carried its message back to Russia word for word', according to Victor Serge. 'Senior officials, People's Commissars and members of the Central Committee read the *Bulletin* avidly, because savage reality was increasingly confirming the exile's most ominous prophecies.'[4]

Among Trotsky's earliest contacts was Yakov Blumkin, a GPU agent who had been very close to him in earlier years. He carried communications back to the Soviet Union, including to ex-Oppositionist Karl Radek. This was discovered and Blumkin was executed – an ominous outcome, since up to this point no Bolshevik had been executed by Party comrades for political activity.

While a majority of Bolshevik-Leninist Oppositionists had been arrested and sent to prison and internal exile in Siberian 'isolators', scraps from the *Bulletin* made their way to them, and 'they were able to discuss the points raised at some length', according to Serge (who is one of the few who lived for a time in such 'isolators' and survived to tell the tale). He adds that 'some of their deliberations were even carried back to Turkey.' The French historian Pierre Broué notes that a small clandestine group remained operational in the USSR as late as 1932, and that 'the links with the workers had been preserved.'[5]

A growing critical ferment was generated by the so-called 'revolution from above' initiated by Stalin and those gathered around him, which involved policies of rapid industrialization and the forced collectivization of land. This generated terrible suffering and growing discontent among workers and even more among peasants. Uprisings in rural areas and militant strike actions in the factories – generally met with severe repression and violence – spawned the sort of sentiments expressed in one anonymous letter to *Pravda*: 'The masses want Lenin's Party, not Stalin's . . . Stalinist leadership is following a policy that leads to the crushing and impoverishing of the working people. We must openly acknowledge that Lenin's Party is no more. The peasants are experiencing military feudalism.' As early as 1928, the Soviet trade union leader Mikhail Tomsky told Stalin that workers wanted to shoot him, and in 1932 the GPU was arresting workers who were saying such things out loud.[6] Based on reports reaching Prinkipo, Trotsky reflected:

> Among the older generation of Bolsheviks, including those who only yesterday were ardent Stalinists, can be observed the complete decay of the authority of Stalin and his group and a decided turn toward greater attention and estimation of the Left Opposition. It is most significant that precisely the Old Bolsheviks, who took an active part in the life of the party under Lenin but later let themselves be scared by the specter of 'Trotskyism', now, after their experience with the Stalinist regime, begin to discover where the truth lies.[7]

It was by no means simply 'Trotskyists' who were opposed to Stalin's policies, according to historians. In 1932 'Party criticism of Stalin was at a high point, especially among Old Bolsheviks of all political stripes', Charters Wynn has observed, with the growing conviction, according to Oleg Naumov and Oleg Khlevniuk, that he was 'incapable of leading the country out of the crisis or placating the peasantry and that, for these reasons, he had to go'. The most detailed critique of the Stalin regime circulating in Communist circles within the Soviet Union was 'Stalin and the Crisis of Proletarian Dictatorship', written by Martemian N. Riutin, who as the head of the Moscow Communist Party and one of the 'ardent Stalinists' Trotsky referred to had played a leading role in defeating and destroying the United Opposition in 1926–7. Stalin's young wife, Nadezhda Alliluyeva, a dedicated Communist, is said to have left a copy of the Riutin document by her side when she shot herself, the day after the fifteenth anniversary of the Bolshevik Revolution, following a sharp public argument with her husband.

('She left me like an enemy!' Stalin bitterly commented.) What was commonly known as the Riutin Platform, while not uncritical of Trotsky, concluded that Trotsky had been 'more honest and dedicated to the cause of proletarian revolution' than Stalin, and 'turned out, on the whole, to be correct' regarding the process taking place within the Party – intensifying bureaucratization and the crystallization of Stalin's 'personal dictatorship in the Party'. In fact, 'the whole policy of Stalin and the party apparatus is anti-Leninist, inimical to the masses of the party members and the workers', having been converted 'into an organ standing above the masses and hostile to them, an organ which by advantage chastises and terrorizes them'. Riutin urged that 'the masses be rallied by the Party' for the purposes of 'putting an end to Stalin the dictator and his clique'.[8]

This document was not the product of a lone individual but of a group, connected with other groups, and exploring possibilities of putting together a broader force within the Communist Party that might depose Stalin. There were discussions among former oppositionists (including Zinoviev and Kamenev, as well as some prominent 'capitulators' from the Bolshevik-Leninists of the late 1920s) and members of the more recent 'Right Opposition' around Bukharin, Rykov and Tomsky, as well as some disaffected Stalinists such as Vissarion V. Lominadze and Sergei Syrstov. An embryonic opposition bloc that would work to dislodge Stalin and democratize the Party seemed a possibility. Trotsky and Sedov were involved in discussions with these currents.[9] Such stirrings were revealed by the GPU in 1932, and intensified repressions soon brought an end to Trotsky's contacts in the USSR and his hopes of being able to return to his homeland.

In the same period between 1928 and 1933 there were groups of dissident Communists throughout the world – disturbed by the Stalin regime's increasingly destructive policies, reflected in the functioning of the Communist International – which began to rally to Trotsky. Relatively small but significant clusters of working-class militants and young intellectuals were crystallizing around Left Oppositionist perspectives in a proliferation of countries on all the inhabited continents. 'Our movement was born within the Third International [that is, the Communist International]', as Pierre Frank, one of the early French Left Oppositionists, commented. 'From 1923 to 1933 we fought – within its ranks or outside – as a faction of the Communist International, trying to wrest its leadership from the hands of the centrists and place it once again on the path of revolutionary Marxism.' The fluidity and seemingly hopeful possibilities in the Soviet Union made this approach seem reasonable to Trotsky's co-thinkers up to 1933.[10]

'I don't think there was ever a movement in which the authority of the leader – not authority that was extracted from the membership or imposed on the membership – but which was voluntarily and enthusiastically accepted by the membership – was as great as that which Trotsky had in the Trotskyist movement', reminisced one earlier supporter in the United States, Max Shachtman, in 1970. Explaining that Trotsky was seen by his international comrades as 'the link between yesterday and tomorrow', Shachtman stressed: 'There was no one of sufficient caliber who could, so to speak, share the lineage with him more or less equally.' Co-founder of the U.S. movement James P. Cannon expressed a similar thought in 1940 when he emphasized that 'very few individual comrades have ever met Trotsky face to face, yet everywhere they knew him. In China and across the broad oceans to Chile, Argentina, Brazil. In Australia, in practically every country of Europe. In the United States, Canada, Indochina, South Africa. They never saw him, but the ideas of Trotsky welded them all together in one uniform and firm world movement.' Yet another founding member from the United States, Albert Glotzer, described Trotsky as 'a center' connected to 'a vast amount of literature, papers, magazines, and correspondence from all the organizations, small groups, all factions in the international organizations, and hundreds of individuals'. Reflecting that 'the pressure on him from all sides, intellectual, political, organizational and personal, is hard to measure', Glotzer added critically that Trotsky 'responded to all of it, participated in the problems of all the organizations, far more than was required or than he should have, even in the trivia of factional conflict'. Yet Trotsky obviously believed that engagement with such 'trivia' was no less important for a revolutionary activist than the composition of the theoretical, analytical and historical works to which he devoted so much of his energy. 'In the eleven years of his last exile,' noted Cannon, 'he chained himself to his desk like a galley slave and labored . . . with such energy, such persistence and self-discipline.' But Trotsky needed the essential interplay between writing and movement-building – and indications are that his activist-organizational interventions were often fruitful both for the organizations in question and for theorizations regarding revolutionary organization.[11]

This movement and its perspectives are commonly labelled *Trotskyism*, originally a hostile epithet which has assumed validity as a more positive descriptive label. Yet Trotsky was absolutely uninterested in articulating some new 'Trotskyist' doctrine. He was, instead, determined to preserve a revolutionary Marxism consistent with what he saw as a rich and invaluable Bolshevik-Leninist tradition. For Trotsky, of course, these perspectives were not precious artefacts to be preserved in an archive or museum, but rather living theoretical and political traditions to be applied and enriched within the context of an ever-changing world. The way he understood and utilized revolutionary Marxism and the Bolshevik-Leninist tradition, of course, invested them with distinctive qualities, shaped and flavoured by his own personality. The substantial literary output during his Prinkipo years was translated into multiple languages. 'Meticulous as he was, he would check every translation down to the last comma', notes

Serge, 'surrounding himself with documents and reference books before writing a single page, verifying every date and searching for the right word.'[12]

Who He Was

Trotsky's autobiography was an activist resource. It brought to life ideas and experiences that conveyed a revolutionary understanding of past and present, and it pushed against Stalinists and anti-Communists who were lavishing slanders upon him. Yet Isaac Deutscher suggests that post-revolutionary developments were 'still too fresh', and his account 'handicapped by tactical considerations and lack of perspective'. There is a 'wealth of insight, incident, and characterization', as Deutscher notes, yet the discussion of Bolshevism's inner life, with the array of personalities and contending ideas (including of such figures as Zinoviev, Kamenev, Krupskaya, Stalin), 'seems hampered by the apparent need to place himself closest of all to the one who, for Trotsky, was the genuine hero of the Russian Revolution, Lenin'. Nor is this the book for detailed information on Trotsky's fierce inner-party disputes with Lenin in the years leading up to 1917. The biographer Ronald Segal, while emphasizing the rich artistic qualities of the work, puts it nicely when adding that *My Life* 'is like a gallery of windows, of which only some are of clear glass, while others are clouded; still others pasted over with posters; and others again, bricked up'.[13]

The beautifully written chapters about his childhood and youth reveal, perhaps unintentionally, elements of the formation of his character, including a relative lack of affection in his immediate family. We see a genuine respect for his father (a practical-minded farmer who had drifted away from his Jewish faith and built up a successful enterprise) but no clear affection for his mother and little sense of his several siblings. Far more vibrant in the account are the labourers and peasants on and around his father's farm, with whom the young boy formed an emotional connection. Also obvious is the impact of an older cousin and his wife, who visited his father's farm, opening new worlds to this country youth as they gave him a sense of new ideas, literature and vaguely radical politics. He went to live with them in Odessa, with his father's blessing, in order to continue his education.

Much is offered about the early Marxist movement and the personalities of the Socialist International. There are vivid and informative accounts of experience in the revolutionary underground, the revolutionary upsurge of 1905 and Trotsky's leadership of the St Petersburg soviet, the impact of the First World War and his crucial roles in the Russian Revolution and the Civil War. It concludes with aspects of the 1920s inner-party struggles and the beginnings of his final exile. It is an obvious must-read for anyone interested in such things, and the literary quality of *My Life* can make such reading easy and pleasurable. The high point of the memoir, of course, is the Russian Revolution, a topic on which he was preparing a masterpiece.

Understanding the Russian Revolution

The History of the Russian Revolution is one of the essential accounts of that extraordinary turning point in the human experience. The prose of the three massive volumes is animated by brilliant descriptions and insightful formulations. The early chapters introduce the reader to the peculiarities, problems and crises that give rise to the first, semi-spontaneous revolution that overthrew the Tsarist autocracy in February/March 1917, to be replaced by the 'dual power' of the people and the politicians. On the one hand there were democratic councils – soviets – of the labouring masses who had brought the change. On the other there was a quickly thrown-together Provisional Government made up of politicians – land-owning conservatives, pro-capitalist liberals, moderate socialists – who were frightened of the revolutionary upheaval and hoped to head it off, despite flowery speechifying to the contrary. The revolutionary multitudes had wanted an end to Russian participation in the carnage of the First World War, to working-class food shortages and to the land hunger of the peasantry. Yet the soviets contained majorities following the prescriptions of Menshevik and Socialist-Revolutionary leaders who counselled moderation. That meant embracing the Provisional Government, even though its politicians favoured continuing the war effort (ensuring sacrifices and food shortages) and delays in the 'complicated' matter of land reform.

Trotsky shows how initial uncertainty among the Bolsheviks quickly changed after Lenin returned from exile. His 'April Theses' called for the democratic revolution to move forward to a second revolution, led by the working class with support from the peasants, resulting in political power being taken by the insurgent proletariat and moving forward to socialism. This would help to generate similar insurgencies and revolutions in more economically advanced countries where the labouring majorities were similarly oppressed by capitalist exploitation and by the imperialist slaughter of the First World War, and revolutionary Russia would become part of a global effort to create a socialist world. After a brief and decisive internal debate, the Bolsheviks advanced increasingly popular slogans for peace, bread, land and *all* power to the soviets. As growing numbers of workers and soldiers (who were mostly peasants in uniform) began to mobilize around these demands, the Provisional Government felt compelled to reshuffle its personnel – adopting a 'left' face by putting the moderate socialist Alexander Kerensky at its head – while offering a proliferation of empty promises. Kerensky finally took repressive measures against the increasingly militant workers, sailors and soldiers of the cities,

While the Stalin regime minimized and finally erased such images as these, showing Lenin, Trotsky and Kamenev at a mass rally in 1920, a central focus in Trotsky's writings was to convey an accurate account of the 1917 Revolution and early Communist regime.

particularly in the capital of Petrograd. But one of the primary instruments of such repression – General Lavr Kornilov – decided that even moderate socialists like Kerensky were a problem, and that both Provisional Government and soviets should be replaced by a military dictatorship that would 'save Russia' by brutally putting an end to the revolutionary chaos.

A horrified Kerensky reversed his repressive policies, urging that all workers – including the Bolsheviks led by Lenin and Trotsky – mobilize to stop the murderous counter-revolutionary threat. This happened, with Bolsheviks playing an essential role, including sending agitators to win over Kornilov's troops, which melted away and joined the Revolution. The now-discredited Provisional Government lost support from a majority of workers, and the Bolsheviks – joined by a left-wing break-away from the Socialist-Revolutionary Party and radicalizing elements from the Mensheviks – won decisive majorities in the soviets. A revolutionary military committee of the Petrograd Soviet, of which Trotsky had now become the leader, energetically laboured to draw together all necessary elements for a new insurrection – lacking the spontaneity of but enjoying the same massive support involved in the overthrow of Tsarism – that swept aside the Provisional Government and gave all power to the soviets.

The conceptual framework for this literary masterpiece was the theory of permanent revolution that Trotsky had articulated in his 1906 pamphlet *Results and Prospects*, in the wake of the earlier revolutionary upsurge of 1905 that had placed him in the leadership of the St Petersburg Soviet. Yet he went beyond this in the *History* by articulating an even more general framework, a way of comprehending the patterns of history which he called *the law of uneven and combined development.*

Uneven and Combined Development

The French Revolution of 1789 is often seen as the high-point of 'bourgeois-democratic revolution' – sweeping away the vestiges of the feudal mode of production, clearing the way for the full development of capitalism, replacing monarchist absolutism with elected governments. Such 'democratic' revolutions (hitting England and North America even earlier) coincided with the triumph of the capitalist mode of production throughout Europe, as well as other continents. Yet this subsequent transformation took place in a manner that was qualitatively different from the form it took in France – and an understanding of why that was the case, Trotsky believed, would provide a key to understanding history.

There is an obvious and simple law of history that has profoundly important consequences. This is the law of uneven development: different areas and different countries are just that – different. While all of Europe had been dominated by some variety of feudalism, and while all of Europe was affected by the development of the capitalist market, the different regions had their own particular characteristics. For various reasons, technological and cultural and ideological innovations arose first in one area and then had an impact on other areas at different times – leading to uneven development in the history of Europe as a whole.

This leads to another historical law expressed by Trotsky in this way:

Unevenness, the most general law of the historic process, reveals itself most sharply and complexly in the destiny of backward countries. Under the whip of external necessity their backward culture is compelled to make leaps. From the universal law of unevenness thus derives another law which, for the lack of a better name, we may call the law of combined development – by which we mean a drawing together of the different stages of the journey, a combining of separate steps, an amalgam of archaic with more contemporary forms.[14]

Uneven and combined development guaranteed that the dynamics of the bourgeois-democratic revolution, and the transition to a capitalist social order, would be quite different in other parts of Europe and the world than had been the case in France at the end of the eighteenth century. This framed the conceptualization of the theory of permanent revolution, which Trotsky first articulated as an approach for the peculiarities of Russia, but which he now concluded had relevance for the rest of the world.

Permanent Revolution

Marxism fuses a view of history, an engagement with current realities, and a strategic orientation for replacing capitalism with socialism. The dominant interpretation of history shared by Marxists of the early twentieth century went something like this: since the rise of class societies (with small, powerful upper classes of exploiters enriched by vast labouring majority classes), there have been a succession of historical stages characterized by different forms of economy – ancient slave civilizations giving way to feudalism, which has given way to present-day capitalism.

The growth of capitalism was facilitated by democratic revolutions that swept away rule by kings and the power of landed nobles, making way for increasingly democratic republics and market economies. The victory of the capitalists (bourgeoisie) paves the way for the triumph of industrialization and modernization. This creates economic productivity and abundance, making possible a socialist future (a thoroughly democratic society of freedom and plenty, in which there will be no upper and lower class). Capitalism also creates a working-class (proletarian) majority which potentially has an *interest* in, and the *power* required for bringing into being, a socialist future.

Many Marxists consequently believed that there must first be a bourgeois-democratic revolution, followed by industrialization and modernization, before the necessary preconditions for a proletarian-socialist revolution can be created. There was a crying need for such a bourgeois-democratic revolution in an economically 'backward' country such as Russia in the early 1900s, oppressed by the Tsarist autocracy and landed nobility (to which capitalists were subordinated as junior partners), with a small working class and a large impoverished peasantry. Many Marxists concluded that they should fight for the triumph of such a revolution, so that capitalist development could eventually create the economic and political preconditions for a working-class revolution that would eventually bring about socialism.

For some Russian Marxists (the Mensheviks, influenced by 'the father of Russian Marxism', George Plekhanov), this meant building a worker-capitalist alliance to overthrow Tsarism. Lenin and his Bolsheviks – revolutionary Marxists, profoundly sceptical of the revolutionary potential of Russia's capitalists – called instead for a radical worker-peasant alliance that would carry the anti-Tsarist struggle to victory. But even they did not question the 'orthodox' schema: first a distinct bourgeois-democratic revolution paving the way for capitalist development; later – once conditions were ripe – a working-class revolution to bring about socialism.

Yet from a Marxist point of view, this schema provides a theoretical and political puzzle. If the working class is as essential to the democratic revolution as the Mensheviks claimed, and their direct exploiters are the capitalists with whom they are engaged in class struggle that (as the *Communist Manifesto* tells us) is 'constant, now hidden, now open', then how can these mortal enemies be expected to link arms as comrades in a common struggle? And if – as Lenin insisted – the workers must, in fact, turn their backs on the capitalists (in alliance with the peasantry) to overthrow Tsarism, what sense would it make for them in the moment of victory to turn power over to their exploiters?

Some have been inclined to argue that 'Trotsky alone [was able] to cut the Gordian knot of the Marxism of the Second International and to grasp the revolutionary possibilities that lay beyond the dogmatic construction of the democratic Russian revolution which was the unquestioned problematic of *all* other Marxist formulations.' Yet scholars Richard B. Day and Daniel Gaido have recently provided a sharp and persuasive challenge to this: 'Leon Trotsky, while certainly the most famous and brilliant proponent of permanent revolution, was by no means its sole author.' Among these are Karl Kautsky, Alexander Helphand (who used the pen-name Parvus), Rosa Luxemburg, David Riazanov, Franz Mehring – and, one could add, Lenin, with his formulation of 'uninterrupted revolution'. The very phrase 'permanent revolution' as well as essential elements of the theory can be found in the works of Marx and Engels – especially in their writings of 1850 and (with specific reference to Russia) writings of the late 1870s and early 1880s, but also passages from the *Communist Manifesto*.[15]

Trotsky himself insisted that his 'permanent revolution' conception overlapped with the perspectives of other Marxists. Some have characterized this as an effort to 'minimize the originality of his conception' in order to 'play down the supposedly "heretical" nature of the theory of permanent revolution'. In fact Trotsky's comments were grounded less in political expediency than intellectual honesty. Far from being the unique innovation of Leon Trotsky, it is a perspective that flows naturally from the revolutionary conceptualizations inherent in the analyses and methodology of Marx himself. 'Trotsky is deeply committed to one element in classical Marxism,' as Isaac Deutscher has observed, 'its quintessential element: permanent revolution.' Revolutionary-minded theorists and activists – seeking to apply such Marxism to the world around them – will naturally come up with formulations going in a 'permanentist' direction.[16]

In Trotsky's sparkling prose we see several interrelated elements formulated more clearly and boldly. Trotsky's formulation linked the struggle for democracy – freedom of expression, the end of feudal privilege, equal rights for all, rule by the people – with the struggle for socialism, a society in which the great majority of people would own and control the economic resources to allow for the full and free development of all. It also linked the struggle for revolution in Russia with the cause of socialist revolution throughout the world.

Trotsky's version of the theory contained three basic points. (1) The revolutionary struggle for democracy in Russia could only be won under the leadership of the working class, with the support of the peasant majority. (2) This democratic revolution would begin in Russia a transitional period in which all political, social, cultural and economic relations would continue to be in flux, leading in the direction of socialism. (3) This transition would be part of, and would help to advance, and must also be furthered by, an international revolutionary process.[17]

One might go further: permanent revolution has applications in the capitalist heartland, not simply in the periphery. Struggles for genuine democracy, struggles to end militarism and imperialist wars, struggles to defend the environment from the devastation generated by the capital accumulation process, struggles simply to preserve the quality of life for a majority of the people, cannot be secured without the working class coming to power and over-turning capitalism. Such struggles in the here and now also have a 'permanentist' dynamic. Nor can the revolutionary resolution

Trotsky at home on Prinkipo, working at his desk.

be secured without the spread of such revolutions to other lands. Trotsky insisted on 'the permanent character of revolution as such, regardless of whether it is a backward country that is involved, which only yesterday accomplished its democratic revolution, or an old capitalist country which already has behind it a long epoch of democracy and parliamentarism', adding:

> The completion of the socialist revolution within national limits is unthinkable. . . . The socialist revolution begins on the national arena, it unfolds on the international arena, and is completed on the world arena. Thus, the socialist revolution becomes a permanent revolution in a newer and broader sense of the word; it attains completion only in the final victory of the new society on our entire planet.[18]

But, again, this is plain Marxism, not some innovative theoretical twist of Trotsky's. He never claimed otherwise.[19]

After Lenin's death, the rising bureaucratic party and state apparatus headed by Stalin instinctively gravitated toward a variant of 'Marxism' that snapped all of the threads connecting the essential elements of Trotsky's formulation of permanent revolution: connections between democracy, socialism and internationalism. Stalin advanced the notion that some kind of 'socialism' (burdened by scarcity and authoritarianism, which would eventually fade away if all loyal comrades did what they were told) could be created in the Soviet Union itself, within a capitalist-dominated world. Flowing from this was the notion that Communist parties in other countries should struggle for democracy and social reforms, but *not* socialist revolution if alliances could be made with 'progressive capitalists' and regimes willing to peacefully coexist with the Soviet Union.

Stalin and Hitler

From 1929 to 1934, Stalin and his co-thinkers engineered an about-face in their pragmatic accommodation when, with the devastating downturn in the global capitalist economy, hopes rose that there might be an international upsurge of proletarian revolution. This resulted in a so-called 'left turn' which, if anything, highlighted the disastrous intensification of authoritarianism that was being bestowed upon the world Communist movement.

Trotsky had an advantage over such revolutionary Marxist contemporaries as Lenin and Luxemburg: the banal fact that he was able to live longer, enabling him to apply Marxist analysis to the most horrific tyrannies of the twentieth century, Stalinism and fascism (particularly fascism's most virulent form, Nazism).

Yet the tyranny with which he was most familiar was the one that he seriously misjudged. At least initially, he saw the brutal

Stalin as being further to the left than the moderate Bukharin, wrongly viewed trumped-up show trials of so-called 'wreckers' among former Mensheviks in the early 1930s as valid measures against actual sabotage, and failed to comprehend the scale of the destructive and murderous brutality against the peasantry involved in Stalin's 'revolution from above'.

Still, early on he got much of it right. Describing the typical functionary of the Soviet bureaucracy, 'who manipulates the general line [of the Party] like a fireman his hose', Trotsky was merciless: 'He eats and guzzles and procreates and grows himself a respectable potbelly. He lays down the law with a sonorous voice, handpicks from below people faithful to him, remains faithful to his superiors, prohibits others from criticizing himself, and sees in all this the gist of the general line.' A few million such bureaucrats constituted the governing apparatus, he added, and a majority of them 'never participated in the class struggle, which is bound up with sacrifices, self-denials, and dangers . . . They are backed by the state power. It assures them their livelihood and raises them considerably above the surrounding masses.' Using the analogy of the bureaucratization of the top layers of trade unions and working-class political parties, raising themselves above the class they claim to represent, Trotsky argued that 'the ruling and uncontrolled position of the Soviet bureaucracy is conducive to a psychology which in many ways is directly contradictory to the psychology of a proletarian revolutionist. Its own aims and combinations in domestic as well as international politics are placed by the bureaucracy above the tasks of the revolutionary education of the masses and have no connection with the tasks of international revolution.' Consequently 'the interests and the psychology of the prosperous peasant, engineer, administrator, Chinese bourgeois intellectual, and British trade-union functionary were much closer and more comprehensible to it than the psychology and the needs of the unskilled laborer, the peasant poor, the Chinese national masses in revolt, the British strikers, etc.' His analysis is summed up with a single conceptually packed sentence:

> On the foundation of the dictatorship of the proletariat – in a backward country, surrounded by capitalism – for the first time a powerful bureaucratic apparatus has been created from among the upper layers of the workers, that is raised above the masses, that lays down the law to them, that has at its disposal colossal resources, that is bound together by an inner mutual responsibility, and that intrudes into the policies of a workers' government its own interests, methods, and regulations.[20]

Far from portraying Stalinism as the product of an evil genius, then, Trotsky sees it as related to the more general development of a bureaucratic-conservative dynamic naturally deriving from historical circumstances and conditioned by specific economic realities, involving an analytical methodology quite recognizable to Marx. Nazism, and fascism in general, are similarly analysed through the employment of basic Marxist categories.

In retrospect one might be inclined to stress that both Stalin and Hitler, while perhaps not geniuses, were incredibly capable, each in their own way (if not in all ways), and that both exhibited qualities to which the label of 'evil' arguably applies. Together they headed the most horrific tyrannies of the twentieth century, destroying the lives of millions of human beings and the hopes of humanity for the realization of freedom and social justice (liberty and justice for all) that had been the most glowing promise of the Enlightenment. In 1932 the urgency of stopping Hitler and the Nazi movement was absolutely clear to Trotsky, as were aspects of the complex link between Stalinism and Hitlerism.

Stalin's dictatorship resulted from the failure of socialist revolution to spread beyond the confines of what had been the huge and backward Russian Empire, involving a retreat from Bolshevism's original revolutionary-internationalist expectations. The resulting authoritarian bureaucracy, which dominated the entire Communist International, adhered to a shallow pragmatism characteristic of such regimes. When a global economic depression began to devastate the capitalist world in 1929, revolutionary hopes ballooned among the bureaucrats, but were applied in a mechanistic and bureaucratic manner.

A theory of three 'periods' was advanced – the first period (1917–22) had been one of revolutionary upheaval, the second (1922–9) of revolutionary ebb and capitalist re-stabilization, and the new third period, opening with the Great Depression, would usher in capitalist collapse and revolutionary triumph. The future belonged to the world Communist movement headed by Comrade Stalin – but a far greater threat than fascists and Nazis (seen as foolish demagogues who would prove helpless in the face of history's revolutionary tidal wave) were currents in the workers' movement that were not part of the Stalinist mainstream. Such elements threatened to mislead the workers, drawing them away from the true revolutionary leadership. This meant they were, ultimately and objectively, twins of the fascists – instead of socialists, they should be considered 'social-fascists'.

Street fighting between German Communists and Nazis became a daily routine in the early 1930s, but an alliance with the massive German Social-Democratic Party – 'social-fascists' – against the Nazis was unthinkable. And if the Nazis took power, the masses would soon turn against them, leading to Communist triumph: 'After Hitler – our turn!' This outlook harmonized well with the fierce and brutalizing industrialization-collectivization policies in the USSR associated with Stalin's murderous 'revolution from above' of 1928–34.

For Trotsky the rise of Nazism could be explained by several convergent developments. Nazism's growing mass base came largely from what he viewed as 'petty bourgeois' layers – farmers, shopkeepers, civil servants and white-collar employees who definitely did not want to be 'proletarianized' and were becoming increasingly desperate for an alternative to the grim status quo and the deepening economic crisis. They, and some 'backward' layers of the working class, were for various reasons alienated from the 'Marxism' associated with both the massive German Communist Party and the even more massive Social-Democratic Party, rooted in majority sectors of the country's working class. Elements from these alienated social sectors were drawn to a plebeian movement steeped in the ideological witch's brew of super-patriotic nationalism and racism that was prevalent in much of late nineteenth-century and early twentieth-century Germany, blended with vague anti-capitalist rhetoric and fierce anti-Semitism. The Nazis drew considerable material support from substantial elements within the upper classes (aristocrats, financiers, industrialists) who detested Social-Democrats and trade unions and who genuinely feared the possibility, particularly with the devastating economic downturn, of the sort of Communist revolution that had triumphed in Russia a dozen years before. The mass political movement the Nazis were building provided a counterweight and ultimately a battering ram to smash the Marxist threat.

An essential ingredient in the growth of Nazi mass appeal was the failure of the major parties of the working-class left to provide a revolutionary solution to the problems afflicting society – the Social-Democrats thanks to the reformist and opportunistic moderation of their own bureaucratic leaders and the Communists thanks initially to their woeful inexperience, later compounded by the sectarian blinders of 'third period' Stalinism. To the extent that left-wing organizations and parties proved ineffective and impotent, Trotsky argued, petty bourgeois layers would be vulnerable to fascist appeals, drawing the more conservative layers of the working class along with them – which is exactly what was happening in regard to the Nazi movement, as masses of Germans were attracted by Hitler's sweeping authoritarian certainties. On the other hand, as history had shown (for example, in 1917), to the extent to which revolutionary vanguard layers of the working class were able to mobilize the working class as a whole into effective struggles going in a socialist direction, growing elements of the petty bourgeoisie would be drawn leftward.[21]

Trotsky called for a *united front* of Social-Democrats and Communists (as well as the dissident factions of each), drawing on a conceptualization to which the Communist International of the early 1920s had been won by Lenin, Trotsky himself and others: the notion that a working class divided between reformists and revolutionaries could defend and advance its interests through a fighting unity, the united front, and that within this context the revolutionaries, as the most effective fighters, could ultimately win the adherence of a working-class majority. This dynamic played out in Russia in 1917, when the reactionary General Kornilov was defeated by united working-class action, in turn giving the Bolsheviks predominant influence in the working class. 'Should the Communist Party be compelled to apply the policy of the united front, this will almost certainly make it possible to beat off the fascist attack', Trotsky argued. 'In its own turn, a serious victory over fascism will clear the road for the dictatorship of the proletariat' – that is, for the working class to take political power and initiate a transition to socialism.[22]

In addition to breaking the Nazi threat and bringing a revolutionary transition in Germany, such a revolutionary development would likely generate similar revolutionary upsurges and transitions elsewhere, and, by ending the USSR's isolation, thereby also help to overcome the influence of Stalinism there and in the world Communist movement. In addition to pushing aside the twin tyrannies of Hitlerism and Stalinism, the question is naturally raised whether such developments might have prevented the Second World War.

Of course, history took a more tragic turn.

Freedom and Tragedy

In January 1931 Trotsky's daughter Zinaida (Zina) and her five-year-old son Seva landed on Prinkipo. She had been an active Oppositionist, as was her husband, Platon Volkov, who remained behind in the Soviet Union. She was only permitted to take one child with her, so she left her older daughter with her husband. By all accounts Zina was intelligent, politically knowledgeable, vibrant to the point of being highly strung. She physically resembled her father, whom she adored. She was also unwell, suffering from a tubercular condition (the Soviet government had given her permission to go abroad for treatment) and from emotional instability.

While Trotsky and Natalia welcomed her warmly, Zina's hopes about forming a close relationship with her father, and about becoming a central figure in his political work, were destined to be disappointed. Trotsky, immersed in the demanding routine he had established for his exile, and subject to the dynamics of his own personality, was incapable of providing the substantial emotional support for which she hungered. Nor did he feel he could entrust her with the confidential political work through which she had hoped to assist him. She was unable to avoid resentful feelings toward her half-brother Lev Sedov (Lyova) and toward Natalia, and there was general agreement among those in and around the Trotsky household – which appeared to have a caring attitude toward her – that her mental-emotional condition was visibly deteriorating. Eleven months after she had arrived with so much hope, Zina finally agreed to

Daughter Zinaida (Zina) visited Trotsky in earlier years, then, full of hope, joined him in 1931.

a move to Berlin for psychiatric treatment, leaving little Seva in the grandparents' care.

But first a new calamity struck: a coal from a wood-fired hot-water heater fell on the wooden floor and set it ablaze. The archives and the manuscripts of *The History of the Russian Revolution* were saved, but much of Trotsky's library was destroyed, and preliminary work on a study of Marx and Engels was lost. After the entourage moved to new quarters, concerns flared when there was another fire. Since Trotsky was insistent, at this time, that Zina get professional help in Berlin, some biographers speculate that Zina set the fires. Trotsky's grandson confirms an earlier account: it turns out that little Seva had been playing with matches, and there were relieved jokes about 'the little GPU agent'.[23]

Trotsky desired, at various points, to be able to visit or live in a part of Europe that was less isolated than Istanbul. Suddenly an opportunity presented itself: an invitation to give a major presentation in Copenhagen on the fifteenth anniversary of the Bolshevik Revolution, under the sponsorship of a Danish socialist students' organization. Visas were quickly secured, and Trotsky

In 1932 Trotsky's great oratory found its final outlet through an invitation to lecture on the Russian Revolution in Copenhagen.

was able to savour virtual freedom as he travelled through Europe, meeting with many comrades and some journalists, and along the way even doing a little sightseeing with Natalia, visiting the ruins of ancient Pompeii in the shadow of Italy's Mount Vesuvius. In Copenhagen, for the first time since addressing Adolf Joffe's funeral in 1927, the revolutionary orator was able to connect with masses of people, addressing an audience of 2,500 at Copenhagen Stadium. An overview of the Bolshevik Revolution, the theory of uneven and combined development, permanent revolution – all as an alternative to capitalism, reformism, Stalinism – crystallized into a remarkable speech meant to popularize revolutionary Marxism for a new generation, and it has endured as a classic statement of Trotsky's ideas. As one of his secretaries later recalled, upon returning to resume his labours in Istanbul, the revolutionary 'seemed to be full of renewed energy' and 'vigor'.[24]

Only a couple of months would pass before a terrible tragedy struck. Zina could find no peace of mind in Berlin. Amid street battles between Communists and Nazis, she hoped for a workers' revolution, yet something far different was shaping up. There seemed no way for her to find a connection to serious political work. She had hoped her brother Lyova and his companion could help fill the void, but her need was far greater than what they could provide, although Lyova wrote to his father expressing deep concern. Trotsky's and Natalia's anxious telephone calls to Berlin could not prevent a dreadful loneliness from engulfing Zina. The fact that her Soviet citizenship was revoked (this was done in 1932 to all of Trotsky's family living outside of the USSR), cutting off her ability to reconnect with her husband and her daughter, may have contributed to this negative development – although there are indications that she had become involved with another man while in Berlin. Zina wanted her son Seva to join her, but once he arrived she fell apart, suicide ending her unhappy life of 31 years in January 1933.[25]

Devastated by guilt and sorrow, when Trotsky emerged from the seclusion of mourning, his hair was white, with new lines marking his face. 'You, her father, you could have saved her', Zina's mother, Alexandra Sokolovskaya, despairingly admonished him from the USSR. Trotsky sent a long, handwritten response to her by registered mail – but he never received the return receipt to confirm that Alexandra received his letter. In fact, all communication links with people in the USSR were snapped during 1932–3, due to the repression following discovery of the Riutin Platform and of efforts to create a broad oppositional bloc.

Developments in both Germany and the USSR would close off hoped-for possibilities, propelling the world in terrible new directions, and compelling fundamental shifts in Trotsky's practical efforts.

3

The Revolution Betrayed

In the year 1933, the world experienced a grotesque tilt.

Adolf Hitler took power in Germany – not through winning a majority in the elections, but through a decision of the conservative politicians representing the German upper classes to embrace the Nazi party and bring its leaders into the government. 'And the workers were divided into rival factions of embittered Communists and hesitant Social Democrats', Gustav Regler, then a dedicated Communist, later recalled. 'The Swastika was the real victor.'[1] From his powerful new vantage point, the Nazi leader could begin demolishing Communists, Social Democrats, trade unions and much more.

At the same time, inside the Soviet Union, Joseph Stalin – whose policies had facilitated the Nazi victory – demolished the fragile oppositional currents seeking to redeem the revolutionary ideals of the early Communist movement. Their tentative efforts to come together, and the terrible violence of Stalin's so-called 'revolution from above', would soon bring a murderous explosion.

Such developments forced dramatic shifts in Trotsky's orientation, as he dealt with what was becoming an irreversible betrayal of the once vibrant revolutionary promise.

Ground to Stand On

When the opportunity to move from the relative backwater of Istanbul to one of the centres of European ferment – France – presented itself in the summer of 1933, Trotsky seized it. Perhaps he had a premonition that this move would, at best, be a mixed blessing. 'Prinkipo is an island of peace and forgetfulness', he wrote in his diary, shortly before leaving, 'a fine place to work with a pen, particularly during autumn and winter when the island becomes completely deserted and woodcocks appear in the park.' No telephones, no automobiles, 'the braying of the donkey acts soothingly upon the nerves.' As his books and papers were packed away, he saw 'empty shelves yawn in the library', and noted a nest of swallows above the arch of the window, hatching 'a brood which has no interest in French visas'.[2]

Within two years in 'democratic' France, amid the intensified commotion from far larger broods of local fascists and local Stalinists, and a hostile bourgeois press, an increasingly antagonistic government imposed severe restrictions on this revolutionary guest. The French Communist Party took the lead, warning that from France, 'Trotsky can attack the USSR, and attack the Communist Parties of France, Germany and Spain' from 'a strategic position' – but that this 'is bound to arouse the anger of the revolutionary workers of France, in solidarity with their free brothers in the USSR.' The French government issued an expulsion order in 1934, placing Trotsky under strict surveillance until another country would agree to accept him. None seemed willing to do so, creating for Trotsky, as he was to comment more than once in these years – 'a planet without a visa!' He reflected: 'During the last year of my stay in France I was more isolated from the world than I had ever been on Prinkipo.'[3]

An escape hatch seemed to open up in Norway in June 1935, thanks to a newly elected government dominated by a Norwegian

Lev Sedov (Lyova) and Trotsky – whose father–son intimacy blended devotion with tension – in mid-1930s France.

Labour Party which boasted a socialist programme and appeared to adhere to the old principles of working-class solidarity without borders. In Norway as in France, hostility towards Trotsky's presence was mounted from both the right and left of the political spectrum. Trotsky was denounced as a 'mass murderer' and 'an executioner' by conservatives, and the far-right paper of Vidkun Quisling's National Union emphasized Trotsky's Jewish background and denounced the 'smuggling of the revolutionary agent, Bronstein-Trotsky, into Norway'. On the other hand, Norway's Communist Party flogged Trotsky for 'opening the sewer for the most vile attacks against the

Soviet Union' and asked whether the Labour Party really wanted to consider this enemy of the working class a comrade. Increasingly feeling pressure from its sizeable Soviet neighbour, the Labour Party's 'socialist' government became visibly uncomfortable with its initial decision to offer Trotsky a home in Norway. Greater restrictions were imposed on his freedom of movement and speech than had existed in France or Turkey – interning the Trotsky household in an out-of-the-way location under a sizeable police guard. 'We simply had to leave Norway, once so hospitable but now our prison', Natalia recounted. 'But where could we go?'[4] By 1937 it would become necessary to leave Europe altogether.

Trotsky's quest for ground on which to stand in these years was not only geographic but also political. In France, in Norway and beyond, it would become necessary to define a new political terrain that would allow the further development of revolutionary Marxist perspectives.

Toward the Fourth International

In 1933 the German Communist Party and the Communist International had failed to provide serious and effective leadership in the struggle against Hitler's coming to power. And now they doggedly refused to acknowledge their responsibility for this terrible defeat. Trotsky concluded that there was no hope of reforming the Communist International or its member parties – it would be necessary to begin building revolutionary alternatives. This had obvious implications, as well, for the Communist Party of the Soviet Union, and for the regime that controlled the USSR, since these had been responsible for establishing and enforcing the disastrous political line that had led to the defeat. Combined with this was the fact that the possibilities for democratic reform in the USSR were being eliminated by the Stalin regime. The increasingly authoritarian and privileged bureaucracy had become an immense obstacle to workers' democracy and revolutionary policy. It threatened the economic and social gains that had been made as a result of the Revolution of 1917. The labouring majority of the USSR, Trotsky now concluded, would need to carry out a *political revolution* – that is, would once again need to take political power into its own hands, and establish democratic structures to hold on to that power – in order to save the situation.

Much of Trotsky's energy now became devoted to helping forge what he hoped would be an effective revolutionary alternative to the Stalinist disaster that the world Communist movement had become. He naturally turned his attention to the possibility of creating an international mass movement whose beginnings might come out of significant forces in and around the workers' movement that seemed to be shifting in a revolutionary direction.

The economic crisis of the Great Depression was causing substantial currents in and around the Socialist and Labour Parties to pull leftwards, away from the reformism of the Second International. The crisis of the world Communist movement had resulted in a number of dissident organizations that found themselves outside the Third International – some not considering themselves in any way 'Trotskyist', some influenced by Bukharin. There were forces, initially drawn to Trotsky's perspectives, that were beginning to develop their own distinctive orientations on various questions – substantial currents led by Henk Sneevliet in Holland and Andrés Nin in Spain, for example. At first Trotsky hoped that a somewhat diverse but basically revolutionary crystallization of all these forces could result in a Fourth International with a mass base. Yet the dissident fragments often veered toward a 'centrist' accommodation to the powerful influences of the Second and Third Internationals at the expense of revolutionary Marxist principles, and they pulled back from the effort to create a Fourth Internationalist alternative.

If there was to be a Fourth International, Trotsky concluded, it would have to be created by those gathered around Trotsky himself, and the Bolshevik-Leninist ideas and perspectives he symbolized. Some objected that relative handfuls of Trotskyists simply could not set themselves up as a new working-class International – they would be isolated from the actual workers' movement and become a sect with decreasing relevance for real-world politics, incapable of moving beyond revolutionary rhetoric and posturing. Trotsky and those who agreed with him argued that there was no serious alternative for revolutionaries, given the political bankruptcy of authoritarian Stalinism and reformist Social Democracy. And if revolutionary Marxist perspectives did, in fact, retain their validity, then over time – based on actual experience and struggle – an accumulation of activists, and proliferating fragments from the ruins of the Second and Third Internationals, would rally to the banner of the Fourth International. But this could only happen if the banner was actually unfurled.

Trotsky was keenly aware of the meagreness of the forces inclined to help build such a Fourth International in 1935 and 1936. He also understood that radicalizing workers and youths, under the hammer blows of the Great Depression, would be drawn to the larger organizations that claimed to pose an alternative to capitalism – the already sizeable Communist and Socialist Parties – not the small groups of revolutionary socialists. Because of this he favoured an 'entryist' tactic in which Trotskyists would enter the larger organizations (this was obviously more possible with affiliates of the Second International). Within these the comrades would help build consciousness and struggles around the revolutionary Marxist programme. Ideally such larger organizations could be won to that programme, although it was more likely – assuming the revolutionaries were skilful – that large fragments could be won over before the reformist leaders drove them out. Either way, through such a process a larger base could be accumulated to carry out, in a few years, the official creation of the Fourth International.

Abstractly this might be clear and reasonable, but it was not so simply carried out amid the immense, complex, contradictory, swirling totality of life, animated by multiple dreams and fears and hungers. There were innumerable, divergent cultural and political tugs; and, as always, the ceaseless interaction of very definite egos and vibrant personalities which all too often collided with each other. The small and relatively inexperienced forces inclined to help build a Fourth International had quite limited resources. The political forces hostile to this project, on the other hand, enjoyed substantial means for well-orchestrated propaganda and slander campaigns, as well as an ability to employ severe and sometimes murderous repression, not to mention spying and insidious infiltration. And then there were all the accidents, mistakes, misunderstandings and foibles inseparable from the human experience. It would not be easy to build the Fourth International.

Considering three significant intellectuals of the left gives a sense of the difficulties. Romain Rolland, the Nobel Prize-winning author of an epic about a fictional rebel and musical genius, *Jean-Christophe*, had interceded with the Stalin regime on behalf of the imprisoned Soviet-Belgian Trotskyist writer Victor Serge. Hopes that there might be similar efforts on Trotsky's behalf, at least in regard to his resistance to Stalinist repression, were to be disappointed. Rolland's revolutionary sympathies remained more at the level of publicly proclaimed humanistic ideals than practical activism, and the Soviet Union had become for him a hopeful dream. He shunned with dismay Trotsky's deepening critique as 'vindictive diatribes'.[5]

A younger left-wing novelist close to the Communist movement, André Malraux, had personally witnessed the debacle of Stalin's policy in China, which resulted in the slaughter in 1927 of many idealistic revolutionary militants. He told their story with eloquence and insight in one of the great novels of the twentieth century, *La Condition humaine* (*Man's Fate*). Trotsky praised this work, and Malraux visited him in France. 'He spent some time with LD in his study', Sara Weber recalled. 'In later afternoon I saw him in animated conversation with LD walking away from the house, along the desolate shore.' Jean van Heijenoort accompanied them, later remembering 'Malraux's nervous, jerky gestures', which 'stood out against the darkening sky, while Trotsky maintained the precise, controlled, didactic gestures of one who explains'. Malraux commented: 'There is one thing that communism will never conquer, and that is death.' Trotsky responded: 'When a man has done the tasks he set himself, when he has done what he wanted to do, death is simple.' That evening, according to Weber, the entire household, with all its young revolutionary volunteer staff, gathered to hear Malraux describe his recent experiences in the colony of French Indochina. 'The parting was warm and very cordial.' And yet the much larger and resource-rich French Communist Party, and the immense left-wing cultural apparatus associated with the world Communist movement, would soon draw the young novelist into the Stalinist milieu, which seemed to provide a better venue for practical action, just as it provided many more opportunities for Romain Rolland to issue idealistic statements to appreciative audiences.[6]

Another intellectual light fleetingly drawn toward Trotsky was the 23-year-old Simone Weil. In 1933 she was associated with far-left currents, arguing that Trotsky and his followers did not go far enough in their critique of developments in the Soviet Union. Trotsky retorted: 'The Left Opposition did not await the revelation of [Hugo] Urbahns, [Lucien] Laurat, [Boris] Souvarine and Simone Weil, etc., before announcing the bureaucracy in all its manifestations corrodes the moral texture of Soviet society, engendering a sharpened, legitimate discontent among the masses and entailing great dangers.' Weil was nonetheless eager to meet

Trotsky and persuaded her parents to offer lodgings in Paris when Trotsky, Natalia Sedova and a couple of comrades were coming to a theatre in her neighbourhood where Eisenstein's film *October* was being shown. Afterward there was animated discussion at Weil's parents' house, with Natalia exclaiming, 'This child is holding her own with Trotsky!' Weil attacked him on the suppression of the Kronstadt rebellion of 1921 and his role in the repressive policies of that time. 'If that's what you think, why do you put us up?' Trotsky asked. 'Do you belong to the Salvation Army?' In their discussion, she was scathingly dismissive of the results of the Revolution of 1917: 'At bottom, LD and Lenin have played a similar role to that of the big capitalists when capitalism was still "progressive" – at the price of crushing thousands of human lives.' She asked: 'What can you give this young generation subjected to brainwashing?' She felt he gave 'an evasive, disheartened reply'. With the continual dismissal of his efforts to provide historical, social and economic contextualizations (rationalizations?) and prognoses (whistling in the dark?), Trotsky exclaimed: 'Why do you have doubts about everything?' This was true of many other, more experienced figures – for example Boris Souvarine, who had begun as a Left Oppositionist, prominent in the French Communist Party, but had broken from Trotsky and was now hailing Simone Weil as 'the only brain the working-class movement has produced in many years'.[7]

Trotsky wrote of her: 'Despairing over the unfortunate "experience" of the dictatorship of the proletariat, Simone Weil has found consolation in a new mission: to defend her personality against society.' Weil's biographer finds this 'a remarkably acute observation', adding: 'Not to be dishonored was certainly one of the chief concerns that guided Simone . . .'.[8] But of course, in his own way, Trotsky saw this as a chief concern in his own life. The fact remained that Simone Weil was one of many talented, energetic, independent-minded iconoclasts to the left of the

Communist Party who could not be counted on to help build a new revolutionary International.

Working with what he had, Trotsky proceeded along what one historian has called 'the rocky road to the Fourth International'.[9]

The People's Front

Trotsky's efforts to build a revolutionary socialist force that could impact upon world politics soon faced new challenges due to a profound shift taking place in the world Communist movement. After a delay of several years, a seventh world congress of the Communist International was held. Pressure had been building up throughout the world, including in member parties, to move beyond the sectarianism of 'third period' Stalinism, with its notions of imminent revolution and of 'social-fascism' blocking the way to effective anti-fascist action. Georgi Dimitrov, the new

The Seventh World Congress of the Communist International (1935) proclaims the People's Front.

head of the Comintern, mapped out before the assembled leaders and representatives of the parties of world Communism a new strategic orientation: 'The toiling masses in a number of capitalist countries are faced with the necessity of making a *definite* choice, and of making it today, not between proletarian dictatorship and bourgeois democracy, but between bourgeois democracy and fascism.'[10]

'The decision was Stalin's', Ernst Fischer, at the time a Comintern functionary on the scene, explained later. 'A Fascist Europe would have placed the Soviet Union in mortal peril. To defend democracy was at one and the same time to defend the Soviet Union.' Or as Louis Fischer, at the time a pro-Soviet journalist from the United States, put it, 'the Comintern realistically recognized in 1935 that the impending war could only be prevented if the Communists forsook active advocacy of revolution and extended their hand to all parties and persons who want to stop fascist aggression', which meant 'an acceptance of the social status quo in capitalist states'. Later historians have agreed. E. H. Carr has noted that 'Lenin's "united front" had been designed to hasten the advent of the proletarian revolution', while 'Dimitrov's "popular front" was designed to keep the proletarian revolution in abeyance in order to deal with the pressing emergency of Fascism', adding: 'care was taken not to ruffle the susceptibilities of those imperialist Powers whose support the Comintern was seeking to woo for the anti-Fascist front.' Paolo Spriano has emphasized that 'although the policy . . . was most closely associated with the International's most prestigious leaders, Dimitrov and [Palmiro] Togliatti, who had recently risen to positions of great responsibility in the organization, its real architect was Stalin himself.'[11]

It was, Spriano explains, 'a great political turn which was welcomed, supported, and driven forward by masses of workers, peasants, and members of the middle class' (the last term referring to professionals, more or less *declassé* intellectuals and artists, small business people). 'Communism had acquired a new countenance: it spoke with a different voice', one which echoed the profoundly humanistic, rational, libertarian and egalitarian qualities of the Enlightenment – emphasizing the virtues of 'the people', the promise of expanding democracy and the prospect of social reforms that would raise up the oppressed and downtrodden in a manner beneficial to the whole of society.[12]

'Apart from the question of whether the policy of the "People's Front" is good or bad', Trotsky reflected, 'it happens to be the traditional policy of Menshevism against which Lenin fought all his life. It signals the renunciation of proletarian revolution in favor of conservative bourgeois democracy.' The exiled Menshevik leader Theodore Dan agreed, expressing regret that in 1917 'it was not the "People's Front" conception of [Menshevik leader] Martov, but the "dictatorial" conception of Lenin . . . that won complete and decisive victory' in Russia.[13]

Trotsky felt that the People's Front approach blurred and made incoherent any pretence at a Marxist understanding of current realities, insisting that it could not realize its own stated goals of stopping fascism and war. He had always championed the working-class united front, whose primary purpose was to facilitate working-class victories around specific struggles, while enabling the revolutionary socialists in such an alliance to expand and enhance their own influence, with a perspective of drawing more and more sectors of the working class in a revolutionary socialist direction. The primary purpose of the People's Front was to form electoral coalitions of working-class parties (Communists, Socialists or Social Democrats) with pro-capitalist liberal parties for the purpose of winning elections and forming governments that, while initiating social reforms, would preserve a democratic republic along with a capitalist economy, and maintain a pro-Soviet foreign policy – thereby (presumably) blocking fascism. In France and Spain such governments were established. The problem with this, Trotsky argued, is that fascism arose out of the crises of capitalism, just as imperialism and war arise out of the natural dynamics of capitalism. To preserve the unity of the People's Front, it was necessary to repress the uncompromising militancy of working-class struggles – but this was the force needed to end both capitalism and the threat of fascism.[14]

Despite the revolutionary clarity provided by this critique, it placed Trotsky and his comrades outside the broad coming-together of progressive forces, including majority sectors of the working class, that rallied to the People's Front. In any event such exclusion would have been insisted on by the Stalinists who were at the heart of this convergence, especially given the repressive developments that were unfolding in the USSR. This highlights a contradiction of the People's Front. If Communists glorified democracy outside the USSR, what explained its absence inside the USSR?

The Revolution Betrayed

If Marxism was to be considered a valid, 'scientific' mode of analysis, the analytical categories developed by Marx had to be capable of explaining how and why a bureaucratic tyranny resulted from the Bolshevik upsurge that had been carried out according to revolutionary Marxist perspectives. This was the purpose of the major work that Trotsky produced in this period – *The Revolution Betrayed*.

Trotsky cited Marx's words from *The German Ideology* (1845): 'A development of the productive forces is the absolutely necessary practical premise [of Communism], because without it want is generalized, and with want the struggle for necessities begins again, and that means that all the old crap must revive.' Marx never developed this idea further, Trotsky wrote, because 'he never foresaw a proletarian revolution in a backward country.'

Nor was it a problem that Lenin dealt with, since 'he did not foresee so prolonged an isolation of the Soviet state.' When Marx speculated about the possibility of a socialist revolution in backward Russia, and when Lenin called for precisely that in 1917, it was with the understanding (as Marx and Engels had stressed in their preface of 1882 to the *Communist Manifesto*) that 'the Russian revolution becomes the signal for the proletarian revolution in the [economically advanced] West, so that the two complement each other', allowing for the socialist development of each. As we have seen, this internationalist element was decisive in Trotsky's theory of permanent revolution.[15]

Yet the revolutionary upsurges after the First World War 'did not lead to the victory of socialism in Europe', Trotsky noted, because the reformists of the Second International – particularly in Germany, where soon-to-be-murdered Rosa Luxemburg and her comrades were assembling forces for revolutionary action – made deals that 'rescued the bourgeoisie'. And what had seemed 'a short "breathing spell"' for world capitalism 'has stretched out to a whole historical epoch'. Trotsky argued that the USSR's contradictory social structure and 'the ultra-bureaucratic character of its state' flowed from this isolation in the global capitalist economy, a 'historical pause . . . which has at the same time led in the capitalist countries to fascism or the pre-fascist reaction'. This led to precisely the kind of situation Marx had referred to in 1845. 'When there is enough goods in a store, the purchasers can come whenever they want to. When there is little goods, the purchasers are compelled to stand in line', Trotsky explained. This led to the next link: 'When the lines are very long, it is necessary to appoint a policeman to keep order.' This simple example, he argued, 'is the starting point of the power of the Soviet bureaucracy. It "knows" who is to get something and who has to wait.'[16]

The growing apparatus overseeing the functioning of the economy – despite the initial egalitarian norms and policies of the early Bolshevik regime – increasingly became corrupted. 'Nobody who has wealth to distribute ever omits himself', Trotsky commented. Reasons and rationalizations proliferated to foster growing inequalities and bureaucratic privileges:

> Limousines for the 'activists,' fine perfumes for 'our women,' margarine for the workers, stores 'de luxe' for the gentry [that is, special shops for the bureaucratic elite], a look at delicacies through the store windows for the plebs – such socialism cannot but seem to the masses a new re-facing of capitalism, and they are not far wrong. On a basis of 'generalized want', the struggle for the means of subsistence threatens to resurrect 'all the old crap', and is partially resurrecting it at every step.[17]

The Revolution Betrayed covered a broad array of economic, social, political and cultural issues. Trotsky went on to argue that the Soviet state and society were fluid and transitional, and could not be defined by 'finished social categories' such as 'capitalism' or 'socialism'. Capitalism was governed by profit-driven market relations, an accumulation process inconsistent with the actual dynamics of the USSR. Socialism could not be reduced to a state-owned economy with top-down centralized planning in a single country, even one as large as the USSR – it required genuine democracy and global scope to be viable and consistent with a Marxist understanding of socialism. Instead Trotsky offered this complex characterization:

> The Soviet Union is a contradictory society halfway between capitalism and socialism, in which: (a) the productive forces are still far from adequate to give the state property a socialist character; (b) the tendency toward primitive accumulation created by want breaks out through innumerable pores of the planned economy; (c) norms of distribution preserving

a bourgeois character lie at the basis of a new differentiation of society; (d) the economic growth, while slowly bettering the situation of the toilers, promotes a swift formation of privileged strata; (e) exploiting the social antagonisms, a bureaucracy has converted itself into an uncontrolled caste alien to socialism; (f) the social revolution, betrayed by the ruling party, still exists in property relations and in the consciousness of the toiling masses; (g) a further development of the accumulating contradictions can as well lead to socialism as back to capitalism; (h) on the road to capitalism the counterrevolution would have to break the resistance of the workers; (i) on the road to socialism the workers would have to overthrow the bureaucracy. In the last analysis, the question will be decided by a struggle of living social forces, both on the national and the world arena.[18]

Trotsky believed that 'only hypotheses are possible' regarding future developments beyond this transitional stage. One possibility was the eventual restoration of capitalism. He had genuine hopes, however, that the struggles of 'living social forces', including in the Soviet Union, would move forward toward socialism in the foreseeable future. Concluding that 'the bureaucracy can be removed only by a revolutionary force', he noted that 'to prepare this and stand at the head of the masses in a favorable historic situation' would be 'the task of the Soviet section of the Fourth International'. He admitted that 'today it is still weak and driven underground', but added that 'the illegal existence of a party is not nonexistence.'[19] As we shall see, this key assumption was to become almost immediately problematical.

Believing that the political revolution he called for must not substitute one ruling clique with another, he insisted that 'bureaucratic autocracy must give place to Soviet democracy', and offered details of what this would look like. Full freedom of speech and genuinely free elections, with not only a democratization of the Bolshevik party but the freedom for other parties to exist in the re-democratized soviets, would all be crucial, as would the revival of trade unions. 'The bringing of democracy into industry means a radical revision of plans in the interests of the toilers. Free discussion of economic problems will decrease the overhead expense of bureaucratic mistakes and zigzags.' Bureaucratic privileges and high-budget 'show-off' projects would make way for a more equitable sharing of social wealth, with decent housing and other social needs being prioritized. 'The youth will receive the opportunity to breathe freely, criticize, make mistakes, and grow up. Science and art will be freed of their chains.' And naturally, 'foreign policy will return to the traditions of revolutionary internationalism.'[20]

The Great Madness

On 1 December 1934 Leningrad Communist Party leader S. M. Kirov, a central leader of the Communist Party of the Soviet Union and faithful Stalinist, was assassinated. The accused assassin had been connected to oppositionists associated with Zinoviev in the late 1920s. A GPU investigation under Stalin's watchful eye soon resulted in accusations against 50 others, with Zinoviev and Kamenev heading the list. Not all of the accused were willing to do what the thirteen did who were brought into a public show trial in 1936 – confess to being part of a 'Trotskyite-Zinovievite Centre' that existed to perpetrate hideous crimes. Brow-beating interrogations, torture, threats against family members, false promises and more were employed – with many of those refusing to cooperate being shot. Of course most of those who cooperated with the prosecution, when found guilty, were also shot. 'In the Trotskyites and Zinovievites', the new history of the Communist Party of the Soviet Union would explain, 'fascism found faithful

PEOPLE'S COMMISSARIAT OF JUSTICE OF THE U.S.S.R.

REPORT OF COURT PROCEEDINGS

IN THE CASE OF THE

ANTI-SOVIET "BLOC OF RIGHTS AND TROTSKYITES"

Heard Before The

MILITARY COLLEGIUM OF THE
SUPREME COURT OF THE U.S.S.R.

Moscow, March 2-13, 1938

IN RE:

N. I. Bukharin, A. I. Rykov, G. G. Yagoda, N. N. Krestinsky, K. G. Rakovsky, A. P. Rosengoltz, V. I. Ivanov, M. A. Chernov, G. F. Grinko, I. A. Zelensky, S. A. Bessonov, A. Ikramov, F. Khodjayev, V. F. Sharangovich, P. T. Zubarev, P. P. Bulanov, L. G. Levin, D. D. Pletnev, I. N. Kazakov, V. A. Maximov-Dikovsky, P. P. Kryuchkov

Charged with crimes covered by Articles 58¹ᵃ, 58², 58⁷, 58⁸, 58⁹ and 58¹¹ of the Criminal Code of the R.S.F.S.R., and Ivanov, Zelensky and Zubarev, in addition, with crimes covered by Article 58¹³ of the Criminal Code of the R.S.F.S.R.

VERBATIM REPORT

Published by the
PEOPLE'S COMMISSARIAT OF JUSTICE OF THE U.S.S.R.
MOSCOW 1938

This is the last of three volumes of trial testimony (adding up to over 1,500 pages) generated by the Moscow Trials of 1936, 1937 and 1938, in which veteran revolutionaries denounced themselves as counter-revolutionaries, proclaiming that they deserved to be shot.

servants who were ready to spy, sabotage, commit acts of terrorism and diversion, and to work for the defeat of the USSR in order to restore capitalism.' There would be more public trials – of Pyatakov, Radek, Bukharin, Rykov and others – showing that 'the Bukharinites and Trotskyites had long ago joined to form a common band of enemies of the people', engaging 'in a conspiracy against Lenin, the Party and the Soviet state ever since the early days of the October Revolution'. They had murdered Kirov and others, had sought to kill Stalin, had carried out acts of sabotage 'and similar villainies over a period of twenty years . . . at the behest of the espionage services of bourgeois states'.[21]

Louis Fischer, a U.S. left-liberal journalist with close contacts among leading personalities in the Soviet government and Communist Party, and whose pro-Stalin sympathies turned to troubled scepticism, observed:

> The chief defendant in all the three Moscow trials of leading Bolsheviks was Leon Trotsky. Men sat in the dock and made statements and received sentences. Yet Trotsky was the person the court wished to condemn. The edifice of guilt which the state prosecutor André Vyshinsky sought to construct was an enormous leaning skyscraper. Its numerous floors and underground cellars were often connected to one another, but sometimes not. Threads from them all ended in the hand of Trotsky.[22]

A stunning feature of the trials is that the accused seemed to confess fully to all of the charges. Historians were later able to discern traces, in all these charges, of old realities – the United Opposition led by Trotsky and Zinoviev, Bukharin's Right Opposition, the Riutin Platform, tentative explorations in 1932 of possible united action against Stalin. But the charges went far, far beyond any of that – as historian Vadim Rogovin has put it,

10 per cent truth and 90 per cent lies.[23] The Austrian Comintern functionary Ernst Fischer, who wrote pamphlets from Moscow explaining and defending the trials, commented years later that 'it is beyond my comprehension that I could have believed such lunacy', which he described as 'some primeval dragon intruding into a world which invoked Marx and Lenin, reason and the rights of man, a monster with power of speech, spouting the jargon of a demented bureaucracy'.[24] In a poem from 1938, entitled 'Confessions', Victor Serge gave a sense of the immense volume, and the seeming madness, of the self-incriminating testimony:

We have never been what we are,
the faces of our lives are not our own,
the voices that you hear, the voices that have spoken so loudly above
        the storm
are not our own,
nothing you have seen is true,
nothing we have done is true,
we are entirely different.

We have never thought our thoughts,
believed our faith,
willed our will,
today our only truth is despair,
this confession of a mad degeneration,
this fall into blackness,
where faith is renounced and recovered one last time . . .[25]

Prosecutor Vyshinsky concluded his presentation to the court in the first trial: 'I demand, Comrade Judges, that these mad dogs be shot, every one of them!' For each Old Bolshevik in the public show trials, there were many thousands of others who had done

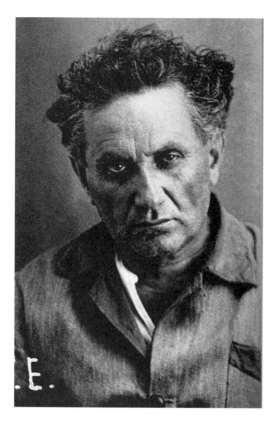

The last photograph of Gregory Zinoviev, who in years past worked closely with Lenin and headed the Communist International, shortly before his execution.

something to make the GPU suspicious or who were denounced by their comrades, arrested and pressured to give names of other 'conspirators' after confessing to their own fictional crimes. 'In the midst of life they cut down workers, writers, teachers, engineers and housewives', commented one of the earliest victims of the Stalinist repression, Maria Joffe. 'They murder fathers and mothers and turn their unfortunate children into waifs, strays and thieves.' It has been estimated that more than 2 million people were condemned from 1934 through 1938 – with more than 700,000 executions (353,074 in 1937, 328,618 in 1938) and over a million were sent to increasingly brutalized labour camps where many more perished (25,400 in 1937, 90,500 in 1938).[26]

Natalia Sedova reminisced about the impact the first Moscow trial (the trial of the thirteen in August 1936) had on Trotsky in Norway:

> By the time we read the indictment in the Soviet press, it was all over. Leon Davidovich, implicated a thousand times over, had not the slightest chance to refute one single lie or to demand proof of one single allegation against him. He was like a man in a delirium during those days, as if plunged into an insane nightmare. He knew all about the corruption and ferocity of the regime and the twisted, but total, devotion of most of the victims of the Party, strangled though it had been by the General Secretary, but their headlong descent into the abyss completely bewildered him.[27]

And yet the analytical framework of Trotsky's *The Revolution Betrayed* provides a basis for making sense of the madness that engulfed the USSR in the late 1930s.

From his 'commanding position in the party oligarchy', biographer Robert C. Tucker recounts, 'Stalin manipulated events in 1928 to make it appear that Soviet Russia was in a state of external and internal emergency that required a policy of revolutionary advance in the construction of socialism, for which speedy collectivization of the peasants was a necessity. He thereby steered the state into the revolution from above.' The impact of this state-imposed 'revolution' was not anticipated by many Communists. 'So habituated was the collective party mind to the idea that building socialism would be an evolutionary process', explains Tucker, 'that Stalin's party colleagues apparently did not divine what the apostle of socialism in one country was saying' when he first hinted at what he had in mind in 1926.[28] It was certainly alien to Lenin's orientation.

It constituted nothing less than a brutal and violent imposition of government policies against and at the expense of the working class and the peasantry.

From 1928 through the 1930s, Stalin's 'revolution from above' pushed through the forced collectivization of land and a rapid industrialization, remorselessly squeezing the working class, choking intellectual and cultural life, killing millions of peasants and culminating in purge trials, mass executions, and a ghastly network of prison camps (the infamous Gulag) that brutally exploited their victims' labour.

There was a method in the madness. What Marx called *primitive capitalist accumulation* – involving massively inhumane means (which included the slave trade and genocide against native peoples, as well as destroying the livelihood of millions of peasants and brutalizing the working class during the early days of industrialization) – had created the basis for a modern capitalist industrial economy. Marx had expected that this capitalist economic development would provide, after a working-class revolution *from below*, the basis for a democratic, humane socialist order. But if Soviet Russia, so incredibly backward economically, was to build socialism in a single impoverished country, then there would be the need to create a modern industrial order through what some had theorized as *primitive socialist accumulation*, the 'revolution from above'. This flowed from the conclusion of Stalin and those around him that – contrary to the initial expectations of Lenin and the Bolsheviks – socialist revolutions in other countries would not come to the aid of the Soviet Republic. Socialism would be built in a single country, the Union of Soviet Socialist Republics.

The effort to regiment agriculture and industry, in order to force sufficient productivity and economic surplus to rapidly modernize the country, generated widespread resistance in factories and villages. This was met with extreme violence and repression against recalcitrant workers, and an often murderous response against peasants – generating a famine that destroyed millions of lives in the early 1930s.

At the same time, an immense propaganda campaign proclaimed that socialism was now being established in the USSR, which involved a personality cult glorifying Stalin. In the new situation the cultural diversity fostered in the 1920s gave way to a cultural conformism under the control of the Stalin leadership. Increasingly literature and the arts – under the heading of 'socialist realism' – were marshalled to explain, justify and idealize government policies.

Ten years earlier there had been substantial oppositional currents in the Communist Party challenging Stalin's authority. Fierce repressions had broken these oppositions, but there had also been very substantial popular discontent. Embryonic developments in 1932 (only four years before the initiation of the Stalinist purges) had indicated the possibility of the heady mixture of popular dissatisfaction coming together with a recomposition of oppositional currents. Russian history had amply demonstrated that small groups could, given unstable circumstances, provide effective rallying points and leadership for revolutionary overturns – which is precisely what Trotsky had helped to lead in 1917 and what he began calling for in 1933. Stalin and those around him, keenly aware of all this, proved quite prepared to initiate what Vadim Rogovin has labelled 'political genocide'.

Destruction of the Soviet Oppositionists

In 1937 small groups of dissident Communist heroes and heroines, the men and women of the Left Opposition, waged their final struggle against the bureaucratic and murderous authoritarianism of the Stalin regime in the USSR, and for the original ideals of the Russian Revolution of 1917.

'When you can no longer serve the cause to which you have dedicated your life – you should give it your death.' These were the words of Adolf Joffe, one of Trotsky's close friends and co-thinkers who had committed suicide as a protest against Stalinism in 1927. His young wife Maria, who had been in the apartment of the Trotsky family when the GPU had come, herself ended up in internal exile in 1929. As the situation of the condemned Oppositionists worsened by degrees, she held out, and when it became the horrific 'one long night' that she describes in her memoir of the late 1930s, she was one of the few who somehow survived to tell what happened. She was sustained by the core belief: 'It is possible to sacrifice your life, but the honour of a person, of a revolutionary – never.'[29]

These self-described Bolshevik-Leninists fiercely embraced and defended the revolutionary internationalism, working-class democracy and uncompromising integrity which they felt had animated the party of Vladimir Ilyich Lenin and the Revolution of 1917, in which many of them had been active participants. Some were younger than that. Adolf Joffe's daughter Nadezhda was twenty-one years old when she plunged into the struggle. 'After my father's death and Trotsky's exile, we developed the Oppositional work with particular force', she recalled. 'In one of his pre-revolutionary articles, Lenin wrote: "We are marching in a compact group along a precipitous and difficult path, firmly holding each other by the hand"', she reflected. 'That is what it was like for us. We were going in a tight group along the edge of a precipice, which was not only deep but fatal for many of those who went.'[30] Like her step-mother, she was arrested in 1929.

As the Stalin regime seemed to be making a 'left' turn, particularly in the direction of rapid industrialization, and some prominent Left Oppositionists were beginning to break ranks, those not prepared to recant circulated the harsh ditty: 'If you miss your family and your teapot too, write a letter to the GPU.' Victor Serge later explained that 'the vocation of defeated revolutionists in a totalitarian state is a hard one. Many abandon you when they see the game is lost. Others, whose personal courage and devotion are above question, think it best to maneuver to adapt themselves to the circumstances.' Christian Rakovsky and two other prominent Oppositionists circulated a declaration meant to rally those among the arrested dissidents who were not inclined to capitulate, yet as Trotsky later commented, 'the ideological life of the Opposition seethed like a cauldron at that time.' Historian Isabelle Longuet notes that some Oppositionists

> attacked [the Rakovsky declaration] for not being critical enough of the capitulators and for overestimating the shift to the Left [by the Stalinists, referred to as 'centrists' by Trotsky in this early period] . . . 'There is nothing to be expected from centrists', they wrote. It was up to the masses themselves (party members and non party) to conquer party democracy and working-class democracy.[31]

Scholars continue to seek a clear understanding of this split among Oppositionists. In a recent essay John Marot identifies a problematical element in the analyses of many Bolshevik-Leninists, including Trotsky to some extent (until 1933). Traditionally to be further 'left' meant to favour greater power in the hands of the great majority of people – but since the early 1920s, Marot notes, Trotsky and most of the top Bolshevik leadership believed that 'the road to socialism' involved 'substituting the political dictatorship of the Communist Party for the democratic self-organization of the working class'. Among some Left Oppositionists, this created the illusion of a positive 'left turn' when Stalin sought greater Communist Party control over the economy. But another scholar,

Thomas Twiss, explains that Stalin's regime adopted 'industrialization and collectivization targets and Comintern policies that were so radical they fell entirely outside of the framework assumed in Trotsky's analysis' while at the same time continuing to 'deviate ever further from the Leninist norms of workers' democracy as Trotsky and the opposition understood them'. In addition thinking among some of the more intransigent Bolshevik-Leninists (communicated to Trotsky, for example, by Victor Serge) contributed to a recasting of Trotsky's critique of Stalinism, with an emphasis on the *centrality* of workers' democracy.[32]

Yet pressures to give in were intense when capitulation could mean freedom, while remaining in Opposition meant never-ending jail and exile. By 1934 Rakovsky himself was ready to capitulate, his views later recounted by Nadezhda Joffe, in whom he confided and whom he won over: 'His basic thoughts were that we had to return to the party in any way possible. He felt that there was undoubtedly a layer in the party which shared our views at heart, but had not decided to voice their agreement. And we could become a kind of common sense core and be able to accomplish something. Left in isolation, he said, they would strangle us like chickens.'[33]

Trotsky rejected this logic, as did many co-thinkers exiled in small village 'isolators'. One survivor recalled the toasts they made on New Year's Day: 'The first toast was to our courageous and long-suffering wives and women comrades, who were sharing our fate. We drank our second toast to the world proletarian revolution. Our third was to our people's freedom and our own liberation from prison.'[34]

Instead they would soon be transferred to the deadly Siberian labour camps into which hundreds of thousands of victims of the 1935–9 purges (including most of the capitulators, plus many other Communist Party members) were sent as Stalinist repression tightened throughout the country. Arrested while in Moscow in 1936, secretary of the Palestinian Communist Party Joseph Berger

Left Oppositionists, celebrating the 11th anniversary of the Russian Revolution in Siberian exile, called for a return to its original principles. Nine years later, under far more brutal circumstances, they continued to organize protests as preparations were made for their annihilation.

later remembered the Left Oppositionists he met during his own ordeal:

> While the great majority had 'capitulated', there remained a hard core of uncompromising Trotskyists, most of them in prisons and camps. They and their families had all been rounded up in the preceding months and concentrated in three large camps – Kolyma, Vorkuta, and Norilsk . . . The majority were experienced revolutionaries who had fought in the Civil War but had joined the Opposition in the early twenties . . . Purists, they feared contamination of their doctrine above all else in the world . . . When I accused the Trotskyists of sectarianism, they said what mattered was 'to keep the banner unsullied'.[35]

Another survivor's account, published in *Socialist Messenger*, the émigré publication of Russian Mensheviks, recalls 'the Orthodox

Trotskyists' of the Vorkuta labour camp who 'were determined to remain faithful to their platform and their leaders', and, 'even though they were in prison, they continued to consider themselves Communists; as for Stalin and his supporters, "the apparatus men", they were characterized as renegades from communism'.[36] Along with their supporters and sympathizers (some of whom had never even been members of the Communist Party), they numbered in the thousands in this area, according to the witness. As word spread of Stalin's show trials designed to frame and execute the Old Bolshevik leaders, and as conditions at the camp deteriorated, 'the entire group of "Orthodox" Trotskyists' came together. The eyewitness remembers the speech of Socrates Gevorkian:

> It is now evident that the group of Stalinist adventurers have completed their counter-revolutionary *coup d'état* in our country. All the progressive conquests of our revolution are in mortal danger. Not twilight shadows but those of the deep black night envelop our country . . . No compromise is possible with the Stalinist traitors and hangmen of the revolution. But before destroying us, Stalin will try to humiliate us as much as he can . . . We are left with only one means of struggle in this unequal battle: the hunger strike . . .[37]

The great majority of prisoners, regardless of political orientation, followed this lead. Lasting from October 1936 to March 1937, the 132-day hunger strike was powerfully effective and forced the camp officials and their superiors to give in to the strikers' demands. 'We had a verbal newspaper, *Truth Behind Bars*', Maria Joffe was told by an Oppositionist who had survived, 'we had little groups – circles, there were a lot of clever, knowledgeable people. Sometimes we issued a satirical leaflet, *The Underdog*. Vilka, our barrack representative, was editor and the illustrations were formed by people against a wall background. Quite a lot of laughing, too, mostly young ones there.' And then 'everything suddenly came to an end.'[38]

In 1938 the Trotskyists of Vorkuta were marched out in batches – men, women, children over the age of twelve – into the surrounding arctic wasteland. 'Their names were checked against a list and then, group by group, they were called out and machine-gunned', writes Joseph Berger. 'Some struggled, shouted slogans and fought the guards to the last.' According to the witness writing in *Socialist Messenger*, as one larger group of about a hundred was led out of the camp to be shot, 'the condemned sang the "Internationale" joined by the voices of hundreds of prisoners remaining in camp.'[39]

Maria Joffe would later reproduce the drunken explanation provided by one of her interrogators, E. I. Kashketin, who had directed the Vorkuta repression in which 2,900 people were killed:

> Those grumbling, accusing theoreticians. Put a bullet in them, that's the only way to get the better of them. Started an 'oral newspaper', if you please – their so-called 'criticism' was nothing but filthy swill poured over everything and anything they fancied. One lot – new professors – dared to 'analyze' and abuse you, at the country's expense, too. Others, under the orders of your 'Vilka', made fun, played the fool. . . . There was nothing illegal or forbidden for that lawless lot. . . . They want everything their own way. . . . They defamed, caricatured Kashketin . . . roared their heads off with laughter. Roared them right off all right – like others before them. And serve them right. . . . Don't you, with all your professors and all your chief trouble-makers in the factories, understand that those who arrive here have already been condemned?[40]

Kashketin was a trusted lieutenant of Nikolai Yezhov, who headed the GPU during the worst of the political genocide. Both would be arrested and eliminated at the end. One survivor of the camps,

Sergei Sedov in earlier years, before he was arrested and pressured to denounce his father and brother as counter-revolutionaries.

Mikhail Baitalsky, recounts that shouts were later heard from a prison window: 'Tell the people that I am Kashketin! I am the one who shot all the enemies of the people at Vorkuta! Tell the people!'[41]

Trotsky's and Natalia's non-political younger son, Sergei Sedov, a mathematician, had been swept up in the arrests. He had refused to denounce his father and older brother and had been sent to the camps, where Joseph Berger met him in 1937. In December 1936 he had arrived in Vorkuta 'and for the first time found himself among followers of his father', Berger recounts. 'They filled him with admiration.' Sergei, still considering himself non-political, 'spoke with veneration of their independence of spirit and could even say that the weeks he had spent among them had been "the happiest in his life." He wanted his parents to hear about their friends and of his own change of heart . . . He was shot a few weeks later.' His parents had imagined the worst upon hearing of his arrest, and now learned of his execution. Trotsky keenly felt his own responsibility for Sergei's plight, speculating: 'Perhaps my death would have saved Sergei.' Natalia later wrote: 'At moments I felt he was sorry to be alive.'[42]

Trotsky's first wife, Alexandra Sokolovskaya, was also remembered by a few who survived the camps. 'Despite her simplicity and humanity', recalled Nadezhda Joffe, 'she seemed to me to be a figure from some ancient Greek tragedy.' When Alexandra heard from another young camp inmate, N. Gagen-Torn, that she had learned something of Trotsky's ideas from an old inmate of another camp, it was 'as if a cloth had wiped the exhaustion and old age from her face – she became young again'. The young comrade agreed to share her message: 'I send greetings to my comrades, I believe in their courage and good spirits . . . Tell them that there, abroad, [Trotsky] will be able to do many things.' Gagen-Torn added: 'She looked at me with radiant eyes, proud of her memories of him, of her love for him. And I, who had yet to understand the tribulations of old age, sat in silent wonder at this woman, and the glow of her reminiscences.'[43] Alexandra Sokolovskaya was executed in 1938 or 1939.

The 'tortures, murders, mass shootings of many thousands of Trotskyists in Vorkuta and Kolyma', Maria Joffe later wrote, moved on to include many more, 'the complete destruction of the October and Civil War generation, "infected by Trotskyist heresy . . .".'[44]

Leaving Europe

Moscow Trials death sentences were demanded and handed down not only for the Old Bolsheviks in the dock, but also for Trotsky and Lev Sedov, *in absentia*. Yet Norway's Labour government was determined to prevent Trotsky from initiating an international campaign aimed at the trials and the Stalin regime. The government was also unhappy with his influence over left-wing elements in and

Trotsky and Natalia in Norway with friends, including generous host Konrad Knudsen (in white shirt). This soon gave way to quarantine and house arrest by an increasingly hostile government.

around the Labour Party, and with the mounting complaints from local fascists and Communists. The solution was to move him to the second floor of a distant house on the edge of a fjord, with fifteen policemen on the ground floor. Correspondence was heavily censored, no visitors were allowed and Trotsky could not leave the grounds. 'The tale of Trotsky's sojourn in Norway reads like a large variation on Ibsen's *Enemy of the People*', Isaac Deutscher has noted. Trotsky himself compared his situation to the fate of the play's hero, Doctor Stockman, 'who was ostracized and hounded for telling the truth' (as the historian Oddvar Høidal puts it), and the country's Labour prime minister, Johan Nygaardsvold, had definitely 'developed an antipathy toward Trotsky' because the revolutionary 'posed a serious impediment to his government's success, in foreign relations as well as domestic politics'. When Trotsky finally departed, the Soviet ambassador appreciatively sent the prime minister a bouquet of pink tulips. As he left, on the other hand, Trotsky accurately predicted that the Labour Party cabinet would itself soon be forced to flee into exile.[45]

4

Bracing for the Storm

The left-wing nationalist government of General Lázaro Cárdenas
– heir to some of the best qualities of the Mexican Revolution –
offered sanctuary to Leon Trotsky in 1937. Key personalities in
efforts to open Mexico's doors to the revolutionary exile included
the artists Diego Rivera and Frida Kahlo. They offered Trotsky and
Natalia a large house, the Casa Azul (Blue House), which belonged
to Kahlo's family. 'It wasn't a soft life we had in that broken-down
villa in Coyoacán, then a backwash village outside Mexico City',
recalled Bernard Wolfe, one of the u.s. Trotskyist secretaries in the
household. 'We lived in a one-story house built around the three
sides of a patio, all of the single-file rooms opening on the internal
garden. There was no heating system. When the panes of the
French doors got broken they didn't get fixed. It turns cold nights
on the Mexico City plateau, up 7,500 feet.'[1] Compared to the
situation in Norway, however, the Trotskys' new place of refuge
must have felt warmer.

As the Trotsky household found sanctuary in the relative
openness of Mexico, decisions were being made in the ussr about
Trotsky's fate. In 1938 a highly placed gpu agent – who apparently
did not care for the decisions – secretly sent a warning to Trotsky:
'As long as L. D. Trotsky is alive, Stalin's role as destroyer of the
Bolshevik old guard is unfinished. It is not enough to pass the
death sentence on Comrade Trotsky, along with Zinoviev, Kamenev,
Bukharin and other victims of the terror. The sentence has to be

Diego Rivera and Frida Kahlo in the early 1930s.

carried out.' Responsibility for carrying out this 'special task' was given to an experienced GPU officer, Sergei Shpigelglas, yet the assignment had yet to be carried when he was executed in the following year. Early in 1939 two other seasoned operatives, Pavel Sudoplatov and Leonid Eitingon, were brought in to organize the killing. Stalin, directly overseeing the matter, made it clear 'he'd had enough of Trotsky's vitriol, of his sway – of his existence.' It was clear that the Second World War would soon begin to unfold. 'He wanted him dead: dead within a year, dead before the war broke out, dead before there could be any question in anyone's mind of his return to the Soviet Union as the more competent war leader.'[2]

In fact, the matter could not be resolved so quickly. Such things take time.

Sanctuary

As with the nationalist revolutionary Kemal Ataturk, although perhaps with keener democratic sensibilities, Mexico's radical populist president Cárdenas felt a natural respect for Trotsky, and despite vociferous objections from right-wing reactionaries denouncing Trotsky as the 'Red Demon' and those in and around the Mexican Communist Party denouncing Trotsky as a vile counter-revolutionary, he wanted to assure Trotsky the kind of freedom and dignity that the Russian revolutionary had enjoyed in Turkey.

Among the Mexicans who rallied to Trotsky, in addition to Rivera and Kahlo, were the writer Antonio Hidalgo, the trade union leader Rodrigo García Treviño, the journalist Adolfo Zamora and the school teacher Octavio Fernández, who was helping to lead the Mexican Trotskyists. The last two, with Rivera, were among those producing a Marxist monthly magazine, *Clave*, of which Trotsky was very supportive. He was especially close to the warm, imaginative Diego Rivera. Van Heijenoort reports: 'Of all the persons I knew around Trotsky from 1932 to 1939, Rivera is the one with whom Trotsky conversed with most warmth and unconstraint.' But he was also eager to connect with the left-wing workers who volunteered to help guard him. Joseph Hansen recalled:

> Among the Mexican guards, some were very poor. They came in their *huaraches*, sandals made of discarded automobile tires, and the gray *serapes* to be seen everywhere in the most poverty stricken areas of Mexico. Trotsky was very appreciative of their participation. Some had to make long trips after a hard day's work. Also it gave him an opportunity to talk with this layer of the population. He enjoyed in particular talking with one comrade who was illiterate. Sometimes they talked for an hour

or more, barely discernible in the dimly lighted patio. His arms clasped under his *serape*, this Mexican worker made no gestures, appearing stolid. Actually he was surprisingly well informed and did not hesitate to express his opinions.[3]

Comrades and supporters from other countries were also, as always, of central importance to the Trotsky household in Mexico. A substantial contingent of secretaries and guards came from the United States, provided by the highly organized Socialist Workers Party, headed by James P. Cannon and Max Shachtman. Cannon had been a long-time activist in the militant Industrial Workers of the World (IWW) before becoming a founder and central leader of the early U.S. Communist Party. The younger Shachtman had been a leader of the Young Communist League and worked with Cannon in the International Labor Defense (ILD) to defend 'class war prisoners', including Nicola Sacco and Bartolemeo Vanzetti. Sacco and Vanzetti were Italian immigrants, and anarchists, arrested in 1921 for a robbery and murder for which they were most likely innocent; yet they were executed in 1927, after a legal process widely seen as biased due to their ethnicity and revolutionary politics. The ILD, set up to defend the civil liberties of militant workers, played a central role in the international campaign that sought to save the pair.[4] Trotsky had deep respect for Cannon as a revolutionary working-class leader, and for Shachtman as an incredibly talented political writer and editor. The reminiscences of both reveal Trotsky's importance to them as well, and the sense of mutual respect that existed in each case. 'There was no bravado in Trotsky — none whatsoever', Shachtman recalled in the early 1960s. 'If anything there was perhaps a sort of fatalism in regard to the possibilities of an assassination.' Trotsky told him: 'It is impossible to work and live in a state of constant terror. We take certain elementary precautions, and that is all we can do.' Shachtman mused:

Behind Trotsky and Natalia, wearing a hat, is Jean van Heijenoort, and on either side are U.S. assistants Joseph Hansen and Rae Spiegel (later known as Raya Dunayevskaya).

As it finally worked out, that is pretty near all that he could do. He could protect himself to the maximum available to an individual or to an individual surrounded by the assistance of people in a very small organization, but that couldn't even begin to be a match for a well-organized assault by an institution with all the power and resources of the Stalinist GPU. Once that institution made its final decision, it was just a matter of time.

Cannon made a similar point in 1940: 'He knew that the super-Borgia in the Kremlin, Cain-Stalin who has destroyed the whole generation of the October Revolution, had marked him for assassination and would succeed sooner or later. That is why he worked so urgently.' Cannon quoted one of the volunteers from the Trotsky household: 'He seemed to be determined to scoop down to the bottom of his mind, and take out everything and give it to the world in his writings.'[5]

This comes through in the recollections of others who were Trotsky's secretaries, such as Rae Spiegel (later known as Raya Dunayevskaya). 'It is his simplicity, the devotion to one cause throughout his life, his fervent belief that the revolution which began in Russia is but a link in the "permanent revolution", the world socialist revolution, that makes of him not a lone exile but a power.' Yet in another comment she seems to have missed a link in what made Trotsky such a power. 'We – his secretariat – felt uncomfortable when he referred to us as his "collaborators." We appreciated his magnanimity but naturally considered the appellation fantastically exaggerated', wrote the young activist. 'But he meant it genuinely enough. He never regarded us as people who worked *for* him. He considered us members of his family who assisted him in his literary creations.' It was another secretary, Joe Hansen, who perceived that more was involved than simply helping Trotsky with his literary creations. 'Trotsky understood to perfection that a party is built through the accumulation and education of cadres.' This is how he understood the decision to build the Fourth International – the drawing together and development of cadres that would be capable of building revolutionary parties capable of forging effective struggles for socialist revolution. He was 'absorbed' by this goal and gave it 'his liveliest attention'. Hansen added: 'For the guards and secretaries, Coyoacán was a school of the Fourth International. All of us followed personal studies which Trotsky, we were aware, noted without intervening', but the education – actually cadre development – went beyond this:

> In a more encompassing way, Trotsky utilized the entire situation, including the organization of our defense, diplomatic relations with the outside, arriving at political decisions,

answering the heavy correspondence, even the articles he wrote, to pass on as much as he could to us from the tradition of the past. There appeared to be no deliberate pedagogy about this; it was just the pattern in which everything was discussed, decided, and carried out.[6]

In this process Trotsky was not interested in the development of yes-men and yes-women, but rather of revolutionaries capable of thinking for themselves. When Harold Robins, a working-class comrade from the u.s., commented that he did not write articles, leaving that to 'the intellectuals', Trotsky admonished: 'How can you say that Comrade Robins? What do you think this struggle is all about?'[7]

Particularly when members of the Fourth Internationalist movement from various countries gathered, there would be 'discussions, sometimes very lively debates – for Trotsky, none of his followers, none who had absorbed his spirit, hesitated to express differences. If they did not express differences, they could expect to be pressed for their opinions just the same.' Again drawing the link between writing and the practical work of building the revolutionary movement, Hansen emphasized: 'For weeks after, a visit of this kind still echoed in the household, one of the indications being a surge in production on Trotsky's broad writing desk.'[8]

One such visit involved intensive discussions with C.L.R. James, the Afro-Caribbean intellectual who had joined the Trotskyist movement in Britain and was now living in the United States. James was carrying out an intensive study of African-American life, racism and the black liberation struggle, involving considerable eyewitness and hands-on engagement. This brought him to conclusions that sharply edged towards a revolutionary black nationalist perspective – which he veered away from in order not to violate the class-focused Marxist precepts that he, along with his comrades, was inclined to

Claude McKay and Max Eastman were both impressed by Trotsky at the Fourth Congress of the Communist International (1922). In the 1930s Eastman would translate some of Trotsky's most famous works, though by the decade's end, like many left-wing intellectuals, he had drifted rightwards in disillusionment.

embrace. Trotsky challenged this veering away and encouraged him to go further in his analysis. James, initially startled, went on to do just that. Interestingly, seventeen years before, in discussions with another Afro-Caribbean intellectual active in the u.s. revolutionary movement, Claude McKay, Trotsky had gone in a similar direction, avoiding 'mawkish sentimentality about black and white brother-hood' and representing an approach which McKay saw as 'more intelligent than any of the other Russian leaders'.[9]

Other visitors were welcomed into the Trotsky household who were not members of the Fourth International. These included Alfred and Marguerite Rosmer, highly principled militants of Trotsky's generation who had been part of the International Left Opposition, then broke away in reaction against a brashly aggressive younger organizer, Raymond Molinier, whom Trotsky initially supported in preference to more experienced cadre among the French Trotskyists. While remaining unaffiliated, they shared many of the old values and perspectives, and remained intimate friends. Otto Rühle and Alice Rühle-Gerstle were also principled militants of Trotsky's generation. Rühle, a former member of the German Reichstag, had, along with another revolutionary socialist, Karl Liebknecht, voted against war credits in the early years of the First World War. But as 'council communists', the Rühles had never been part of the Left Opposition. They too shared some values and perspectives with Trotsky, but nonetheless very sharply differed on major political questions – and yet had also become intimate friends. Rühle, author of a widely read biography of Marx, collaborated with Trotsky on preparing *The Living Thoughts of Karl Marx*, published in the u.s. in 1939. Then there was the Surrealist poet and writer André Breton, whose revolutionary sympathies brought him close to Trotsky. While not inclined to help build a revolutionary party, he was quite prepared to collaborate with Trotsky and Diego Rivera to issue a 'Manifesto for an Independent Revolutionary Art', which asserted that 'the artist cannot serve the struggle for freedom unless he subjectively assimilates its social content, unless he feels in his very nerves its meaning and drama and freely seeks to give his own inner world incarnation in his art.'[10]

War Against Fascism

Spain was a flashpoint in the last half of the 1930s. Immense working-class ferment, punctuated by multiple upsurges, swept aside the centuries-old monarchy, which was replaced by a more or less democratic republic. Big landowners, bankers and industrialists still held economic power and felt threatened – with good reason – as the large anarchist and anarcho-syndicalist movements, the large Socialist Party and the smaller but growing Communist Party reshaped the political terrain. Basque and Catalonian nationalists reaching for autonomy added to the mix, as did the merger of a dynamic Trotskyist group with another dissident Communist faction to form the militant Partido Obrero de Unificacíon Marxista (POUM – Workers' Party of Marxist Unification), which was especially influential in Barcelona. Various conservative, pro-monarchist, reactionary-nationalist, right-wing Catholic and fascist groups were extremely antagonistic to the left, of course, and also to the Republican Action Party, which favoured capitalism but also a liberal political agenda. In 1935 a People's Front coalition of the liberal Republicans, Socialists and Communists (with tacit anarchist support) won a slim majority of the vote and established a government, to the horror of the right-wing forces, which had considerable influence in the upper circles of the military. A military coup was blocked by a general strike and mobilization of the workers. This led to the Spanish Civil War of 1936–9.

The so-called 'nationalists' or 'insurgents' were supported by fascist and right-wing forces throughout the world, receiving considerable aid from Hitler's Germany and Mussolini's Italy. The 'loyalist' defence of the Spanish Republic became a *cause célèbre* of the international left, with the Communist International playing a major role in organizing the International Brigades of idealistic young volunteers from many countries, and the Soviet Union sending significant material aid. But this also gave the Stalin regime significant influence inside Republican Spain, which it utilized to advance People's Front perspectives, Stalinist foreign policy considerations and increasingly repressive policies toward the revolutionary left. Yet such anti-revolutionary policies did nothing to persuade the capitalist 'democracies' to aid the left-liberal Spanish Republic, or to prevent the eventual victory of fascist forces and the installation in 1939 of the dictatorship of Generalissimo Francisco Franco.[11]

Trotsky was critical of the POUM for veering away from the Fourth International, and for giving support to the People's Front electoral pact. It is unlikely, however, that he would have disagreed with what one POUMist said quietly but firmly in a confrontation with members of the International Brigades:

> The only victories against the army, against the Church, against the falangistas [Spanish fascists] had been won by the workers and peasants, while the democratic government had sat on its hands. We can run the factories, and we can run the fields as brothers, they belong to us who do the work. We can manufacture our own arms, what we must do is take over all the factories of Spain. We must give Morocco its freedom and so stop the flow of Moorish mercenaries by Franco. You Communists have given up the fight for socialism, we of the POUM who are free of foreign influence, Stalin is not our leader, we govern ourselves.[12]

Yet in the autumn of 1936, the POUM – along with representatives of the anarcho-syndicalist labour federation – joined the People's Front coalition government in Barcelona. 'The theoreticians for the Popular Front do not essentially go beyond the first rule of arithmetic, that is, addition: "Communists" plus Socialists plus Anarchists plus liberals add up to a total that is greater than their respective isolated numbers', Trotsky wrote. But there was, he insisted, a higher mathematics to consider: 'When political allies pull in opposite directions, the result may prove to be zero.' The pro-capitalist liberals and Stalinists and Social-Democratic reformists were pushing in one direction, in favour of 'democratic' capitalism, whereas the anarchists and revolutionary socialists were pushing in a revolutionary direction – while still trying to maintain an alliance that hampered them from doing just that. 'The renunciation of conquest of power inevitably throws every workers organization into the swamp of reformism and turns it into the toy of the bourgeoisie' – this was true of both the anarchists and the POUM, in Trotsky's opinion. This undermined an effective popular struggle against fascism. As he summed it up:

> I would say, 'No political alliance with the bourgeoisie', as the first condition. The second, 'You must be the best soldiers against the fascists.' Third, 'You must say to the soldiers, to the other soldiers and the peasants: 'We must transform our country into a people's country. Then, when we win the masses, we will throw the bourgeoisie out of office, and then we will be in power and we will make the social revolution.'[13]

Meeting Stalin's Assaults

In Spain and elsewhere an ominous development was taking place in 1937 – the Stalinist movement used systematic violence to eliminate real and imagined competitors and opponents within the workers' movement. Not only were many thousands of Soviet and foreign Communists being destroyed in the USSR in this period, but numerous dissident Communists and others were being murdered in Spain, including anarchists and POUMists, and in other countries as well. The GPU maintained an international network – secretly in touch with a select number of Communist Party members in various countries (though without the knowledge of the overwhelming majority of Communists) – which, among other things, carried out a significant number of killings, beginning at least as early as the spring of 1937. Trotsky responded: 'Stalinism is the syphilis of the workers' movement. Anybody who chances to be a direct or indirect carrier of such contamination should be submitted to a pitiless quarantine. The hour has struck for the unsparing demarcation of honest people from all the agents, friends, lawyers, publicists, and poets of the GPU.'[14]

Isaac Deutscher has suggested that Trotsky may have gone too far, committing 'a minor blunder' in late 1939 by agreeing to testify against Stalinism before the notorious House Un-American Activities Committee, then headed by right-wing congressman Martin Dies. Yet the u.s. Communist Party leaders William Z. Foster and Earl Browder had voluntarily appeared before the Dies Committee in September 1939, where they argued that the 'fascistic' Trotskyites should be forcibly suppressed. When it became known that Trotsky's testimony might include denunciations of the committee and its inclinations to outlaw the Communist Party, the invitation was withdrawn.[15]

Far more effective was the creation in 1937 of an international commission that painstakingly investigated and exposed the fraudulence of the first two Moscow Trials (the third taking place after this commission had concluded its work). The formal name was The Commission of Inquiry into the Charges Made against Leon Trotsky in the Moscow Trials – but it was known more familiarly as the Dewey Commission, because its chairman was the outstanding liberal philosopher and educator John Dewey.[16]

Other members of the commission were Otto Rühle; the liberal u.s. journalists Benjamin Stolberg, Suzanne LaFollette and John Chamberlain (the latter two on a trajectory to conservative libertarianism); Carleton Beals, an authority on Latin-American affairs (with enough sympathies for the Communist Party to feel uncomfortable on the commission, from which he resigned); Alfred Rosmer, an outstanding figure in the French anarcho-syndicalist movement who in 1920–21 had been a member of the Executive Committee of the Communist International; Wendelin Thomas, the leader of the Wilhelmshaven sailors' revolt in November 1918 and later a Communist member of the German Reichstag (and, with Rühle, now a left-libertarian 'council communist'); Edward A. Ross, a professor of sociology at the University of Wisconsin and the author of outstanding early scholarly studies of the Russian Revolution; Carlo Tresca, the well-known Italian-American anarchist leader; and Francisco Zamora, the Mexican journalist. The commission's legal counsel was John Finerty, famous as a defence lawyer in such great American political trials as those of the imprisoned socialist Tom Mooney and the anarchist martyrs Nicola Sacco and Bartolemeo Vanzetti. The critical-minded attitude of such people set them apart from a widespread orientation, predominant among many liberal and left-wing intellectuals at the time, which accepted the validity of the Moscow trials.[17]

The commission members sifted through enormous quantities of evidence and took testimony over a period of months, before declaring on 21 September 1937:

(1) That the conduct of the Moscow trials was such as to convince any unprejudiced person that no effort was made to ascertain the truth. (2) While confessions are necessarily entitled to the most serious consideration, the confessions themselves contain such inherent improbabilities as to convince the Commission that they do not represent the truth, irrespective of any means used to obtain them.[18]

A portion of the commission met in Coyoacán, in the spacious Casa Azul, from 10 to 17 April 1937 in order to take testimony from Trotsky, often with sharp questioning. The Marxist intellectual George Novack, a Socialist Workers Party member who attended as a national secretary of the American Committee for the Defense of Leon Trotsky, recalls that 'Trotsky was subjected to the most searching examination by his attorney and cross-examination by the commission members and their counsel. He had to do more than expose the falsity of Moscow's allegations.' Over a thirteen-day set of hearings, Trotsky 'had to recount the main events of his career, expound his beliefs, describe and explain the bewildering changes that had taken place in the Soviet Union from Lenin to Stalin. He had to analyse the issues in the factional disputes within Russian and world communism, portray the leading personalities in the struggles, and touch upon every phase of the terrible contest between Stalin and himself which led up to the trials', Novack recalled. 'The record of the hearings is therefore an extensive and valuable compendium of information about the events, personalities, and problems of the Russian revolution and the Soviet Union. It presents the ideas and positions of Marxism, Bolshevism, and Trotskyism on a wide range of questions.'[19] A sense of the give-and-take can be gleaned from the following excerpt:

DEWEY: I have a very few questions along the line of the question I asked you the other day, quoting your passage about iron necessity developing the bureaucracy in Russia, considering the backwardness of the country and the lack of revolution, successful revolutions, in other countries. I want to ask you what reason there is for thinking that the dictatorship of the proletariat in any country will not degenerate into the dictatorship of the secretariat.

TROTSKY: It is a very good formula. I must answer that even the dictatorship of the secretariat now in Russia is a very important progress in comparison with the dictatorship of the Tsar. That is the first thing. It signifies that on the eve of the October Revolution, if anybody could have predicted to me the consequences, I would still have accepted it. Because Russia had only the choice between the Kornilov régime and the dictatorship of the proletariat. Secondly, just because the dictatorship of the secretariat is caused by the backwardness of the country and its isolation, the answer is that the more civilized countries, and not isolated, will have a more sound and more democratic dictatorship and for a shorter period.

LAFOLLETTE: May I interrupt? You have planned economy, and how can you avoid having a lot of bureaucrats; how can you avoid having a dictatorship of the secretariat?

TROTSKY: I must repeat the answer suggested to me by Commissioner Otto Rühle: What is the distinction between administration and bureaucracy? The difference is fundamental. The administration has a certain function. In America you name administration also government, if I am correct. But we don't apply this name for government, as administration. I have in my mind the administration of a workers' cooperative, the administration of a good, sound trade union, or the best sometimes that we can find; but they are not bureaucrats, if it has a sound relation between the members and the leaders.[20]

Trotsky concluded his final testimony:

The experience of my life, in which there has been no lack either of successes or of failures, has not only not destroyed my faith in the clear, bright future of mankind, but, on the contrary, has given it an indestructible temper. This faith in reason, in truth, in human solidarity, which at the age of eighteen I took with me into the workers' quarters of the provincial Russian town of Nikolaev – this faith I have preserved fully and completely. It has become more mature, but not less ardent. In the very fact of your Commission's formation – in the fact that, at its head, is a man of unshakable moral authority, a man who by virtue of his age should have the right to remain outside of the skirmishes in the political arena – in this fact I see a new and truly magnificent reinforcement of the revolutionary optimism which constitutes the fundamental element of my life.[21]

Personal Matters

In the wake of the Dewey Commission hearings, there was an unusual (and for the informed few, extremely disturbing) development – a secret romance between Trotsky and Frida Kahlo.[22]

Jean van Heijenoort, a scrupulous and knowledgeable witness, asserts: 'Trotsky's love affair with Frida was, I am certain, the first adventure of this kind that he had engaged in since leaving Russia.' Nadezhda Joffe, a knowledgeable witness from the 1917–27 period, commented that 'any sort of romance is, of course, out of the question, Trotsky simply did not have the time for romances.' Yet she distinguished between romances and 'occasional liaisons', adding 'it is quite likely that among such was an affair with Larisa Reissner.' There are indications of liaisons in the same period with the English sculptor Clare Sheridan and the u.s. journalist Anna Louise Strong.[23] Each was not simply physically attractive but also intelligent, independent-minded, creative – certainly qualities of Frida Kahlo herself, with whom he became utterly infatuated.

The novelist Meaghan Delahunt, reaching beyond what is known, suggests that Trotsky was keenly aware of impending death, drawn to 'the unpredictability of the first night, emotion undulating and uncertain . . . He had seen himself new, had felt as if all the accumulations of his past had been rolled back in the body of a person much younger than himself who knew only the grandeur of him and none of its fading . . . The time with Frida had been the last time he had felt alive to his fingertips.' Lillian Pollak, who was actually on the scene during this period, offers a succinct description that hews to the documented facts, concluding:

> After three months, Frida and Trotsky end their affair. They both recognize that if it continues the resulting scandal could be disastrous. Frida is relieved – she tells a friend 'Estoy muy canasada del Viejo – I am very tired of the Old Man.' Trotsky continues to

write her ardent letters and briefly entertains the idea of making love to Frida's sister, Cristina. But eventually coming to his senses, he turns back to Natalya with tears and apologies, calling her 'my only one, my eternal one, my faithful one, my love, my victim.'[24]

It is hardly the case that Trotsky's passion had grown cold for Natalia, the love of his life, the comrade who had been his most intimate friend. In the wake of his betrayal he laboured to win back the trust of the woman whom he had described in his diary only three years before:

> The radio is playing the *Symphonie héroïque* . . . I envy N. when she is listening to great music: she listens with all the pores of her soul and body. N. is not a musician, but she is something more than that: her whole nature is musical; in her sufferings as well as in her – infrequent – joys, there is always a deep melody which ennobles all her experiences. Even though she is interested in the small daily facts of politics, she does not usually combine them into one coherent picture. Yet when politics go deep down and demand a complete reaction, N. always finds in her inner music the right note. The same is true of her judgments of people, and not only personal, psychological ones, but also those she makes as a revolutionary. Philistinism, vulgarity, and cowardice can never be concealed from her, even though she is exceptionally lenient toward all minor human vices.
>
> Sensitive people, even quite 'simple' people – and children too – instinctively feel the musicality and depth of her nature. Of those who pass her by with indifference or condescension, without noticing the forces concealed in her, one can almost always say with certainty that they are superficial and trivial.[25]

Trotsky regained his friend's acceptance and trust, although she was keenly aware – as she always had been – of his contradictory nature, which she had seen over the years playing itself out in relations with others. This was the case with one of his most trusted assistants, Jean van Heijenoort. 'There were periods of cheerful and warm confidence, followed by moments, often without my understanding the reason for the change, of surliness and tension.' There was no assistant more trusted, however, than Trotsky's older son Lev Sedov (Lyova), who played a central role in the work of the International Left Opposition. And no one suffered more from Trotsky's swings toward 'surliness and tension' than his son.

The relationship included considerable love, trust and pride, as well as an intimacy intertwined with a deep bond of comradeship – sometimes almost an identification of son with self. A consequent blurring of boundaries, impossible expectations and hyper-critical impatience seem to have combined with tendencies related to the deep streak of arrogance noted by so many, an identification of Trotsky's fallible self with the transcendent cause of socialist revolution. All of this was exacerbated ten times over by the intense, overwhelming pressures of his situation in exile that we have been examining here. Natalia records that he confessed to her with considerable depth of feeling during a winter's walk in Norway, even before the Moscow Trials, 'I am tired of it all – all of it – do you understand?'[26] The pressures would get much worse, sometimes causing his negative personal tendencies to surge out of control. This impacted especially on his closest political and literary collaborator, who was central to the intensive work of the International Left Opposition and who oversaw the editing, production and distribution of the *Bulletin of the Opposition*, as well as tending to innumerable tasks related to his father's literary needs (securing books, information and so on) and to the needs of the Trotsky household.

'Papa accuses me not only of dilettantism, but of disorganization, in a certain number of factual questions which simply do not correspond to reality', he wrote to his mother in 1933. 'By reading

Papa's letter written with poison and spite, I felt once more what I had more than once felt before: that it is on the heads of "the best" and those most "worthy of confidence" of those close to him that he places the mark of failure.' Sedov added that this 'can hardly be a good method and does not contribute to the cause (because it oppresses "the best" instead of enabling them to raise themselves up). And in the given case, the tone itself was simply monstrous . . . [and] . . . undermines relationships.' In 1936: 'I think all Dad's deficiencies have not diminished as he grew older but under the influence of his isolation, very difficult, unprecedentedly difficult, gotten worse. His lack of tolerance, hot temper, inconsistency, even rudeness, his desire to humiliate, offend, and even destroy have increased. It is not personal, it is a method, and hardly good in organization work.'[27]

We see here deep filial hurt, but also the observations and concerns of an experienced political organizer. Surveying Trotsky's relationships with hundreds of comrades and the many groups of the International Left Opposition during his long years in exile, one finds incredible patience and insight, political and organizational wisdom, dynamics animated by mutual respect. Inevitably there are also tensions, genuine political and theoretical differences and necessarily sharp conflicts.[28] Yet certain conflicts may also include dynamics to which Sedov points.

In February 1938 Sedov's life was suddenly extinguished under suspicious circumstances. Undergoing an operation for acute appendicitis at a clinic in Paris, where he was living and working, he seemed to be recovering nicely, then suddenly became delirious and died. Some of the personnel at the clinic were Russian émigrés with pro-Soviet ties. One of Sedov's closest political associates, a Soviet émigré named Mark Zborowsky (known in Left Opposition circles as Étienne), was secretly working for the GPU. There was a string of GPU-initiated murders of Trotsky's secretaries – Rudolph Klement, Erwin Wolf, Walter Held. There was also the murder of Ignace Reiss, a GPU operative who was horrified and disgusted with the Stalinist political genocide and who publicly broke from the GPU and declared support for the Fourth International. The best-known Trotskyists in Europe, Reiss had warned, were all marked for assassination. Sedov himself had been condemned to death, *in absentia*, in Soviet courts.[29]

With Lyova's death, 'Leon Davidovich and Natalia Ivanovna locked themselves into their room and would see no one', recorded the devoted secretary Rae Spiegel. 'For a whole week they did not come out of their room, and only one person was permitted in – the maid who brought them the mail, and food, of which they partook little.' When Trotsky emerged on the eighth day, Spiegel 'was petrified at the sight of him. The neat, meticulous Leon Trotsky had not shaved for a whole week. His face was deeply lined. His eyes were swollen from too much crying.' In the handwritten manuscript he brought with him – the glowing tribute and remembrance *Leon Sedov, Son, Friend, fighter* – is the comment: 'together with our boy has died everything that still remained young within us.' Afterwards, Joe Hansen noted a marked change in Trotsky. 'The word that occurred to me was mellowness; yet that was not quite right', Hansen later wrote. 'He did not seem to drive others as hard as he had before. He had more consideration, I felt, for weaknesses in his collaborators. It was subtle but definitely there so that it became a new element in relationships within the household.'[30]

All of Trotsky's children were now dead. All but one of his orphaned grandchildren were in unknown circumstances within the vast land ruled by the murderous regime. At this point it became emotionally imperative for Trotsky and Natalia Sedova to reach out and draw into their home young Seva, the son of Zinaida, who after his mother's death had been cared for by Lev Sedov and his companion Jeanne Martin. The two had experienced a difficult relationship that was made more tense by her adherence to a political split-off among the French Trotskyists in disagreement with some of Trotsky's perspectives. After Sedov's death, Jeanne too felt compelled to cling to Seva, but refused the offer to live with him in the Trotsky household, even after it was legally determined that Seva should live with his grandparents. The personal intervention of Alfred and Marguerite Rosmer finally allowed Trotsky and Natalia to embrace their twelve-year-old grandson as part of their own household.

A Spotless Banner

Small groups of workers and intellectuals throughout the world sought to preserve perspectives that had infused the revolutionary wing of the young Second International and the original founders of the Third International. They joined with Trotsky as part of a global resistance to Stalinism, to help create, to the best of their abilities, a force for socialist revolution. Soon Trotsky was labouring to turn such aspirations and commitments into a new 'world party for socialist revolution' – the Fourth International. In 1935 he sought to place this into historical context:

> The very sequence of the Internationals has its own internal logic, which coincides with the historic rise of the proletariat. The first International advanced the scientific program of the proletarian revolution, but it fell because it lacked a mass base. The Second International dragged from the darkness, educated, and mobilized millions of workers, but in the decisive hour it found itself betrayed by the parliamentary and the trade union bureaucracy corrupted by rising capitalism. The Third International set for the first time the example of the victorious proletarian revolution, but it found itself ground between the millstones of the bureaucracy in the isolated Soviet state and the reformist bureaucracy of the West. Today, under the conditions of decisive capitalist collapse, the Fourth International,

Trotsky and Natalia with their grandson Seva, just brought to them by Alfred and Marguerite Rosmer.

standing upon the shoulders of its predecessors, enriched
by the experience of their victories and defeats, will mobilize
the toilers of the Occident and the Orient for the victorious
assault upon the strongholds of world capital.[31]

With the approach of a cataclysmic Second World War,
Trotsky's insistence upon the creation of the new International
became increasingly urgent. One of those in the Trotskyist
movement who opposed taking this step, Isaac Deutscher, later
commented: 'The Fourth International proved to be a stillbirth,
and this largely because no international revolutionary movement
was there to breathe life into it.' Indeed, four years earlier Trotsky
had expressed his hopes and fears regarding the future Fourth
International: 'It may be constituted in the process of the struggle
against fascism and the victory gained over it. But it may also be
formed considerably later, in a number of years, in the midst of
the ruins and the accumulation of debris following upon the
victory of fascism and war.' Trotsky himself was far from satisfied
with the nature of the groups that would constitute the new
International. His 'perpetual grievance against the Trotskyite
groups was their poor social composition: too many intellectuals,
too few workers', recalled his aide Jean van Heijenoort. 'The only
two Trotskyite groups about which I heard him express unqualified
admiration were the Charleroi group in Belgium, made up of coal
miners, and the Minneapolis group in the United States, made up
of teamsters' – which in 1936 and 1934 respectively played central
roles in general strikes that won working-class victories.[32]

The reflections of Afro-Caribbean intellectual C.L.R. James
in 1940, shortly after Trotsky's death, provide a more positive
anticipation:

Stalin, aware of the state of his regime and in what a tottering
world he lived, did not count Trotsky's meager following and

then sit back in comfort. He knew that as long as Trotsky lived and could write and speak, the Soviet bureaucracy was in mortal danger. In a conversation just before war broke out, Hitler and the French ambassador discussed the perils of plunging Europe into conflict and agreed that the winner of the second great war might be Trotsky. Winston Churchill hated him with a personal malevolence which seemed to overstep the bounds of reason. These men knew his stature, the power of what he stood for, and were never lulled by the smallness of his forces.[33]

Trotsky was unable to attend the founding conference of the Fourth International, which opened in France on 3 September 1938. 'No conference of revolutionists ever met under circumstances more tense and ominous', according to the conference's official report, 'or faced tasks of such supreme historical gravity than did this one.' The participants numbered about 30, representing the United States, France, Great Britain, Germany, the Soviet Union, Italy, Poland, Belgium, Holland and Greece, plus countries in Latin America. In addition, 'unable to send delegates because of conditions of distance, illegality, and other adverse factors were organizations affiliated to the Fourth International in Spain, Czechoslovakia, Austria, Indochina, China, French Morocco, the Union of South Africa, Canada, a number of Latin American countries, Australia, New Zealand, Denmark, Norway, Palestine, Lithuania, Rumania, and several other countries.'[34]

The central document of the founding conference was written by Trotsky, in consultation with various other comrades, particularly in the United States, and was entitled 'The Death Agony of Capitalism and the Tasks of the Fourth International'. Later it would come to be known as the *Transitional Program*. At its conclusion, Trotsky focused on the question: is it time to

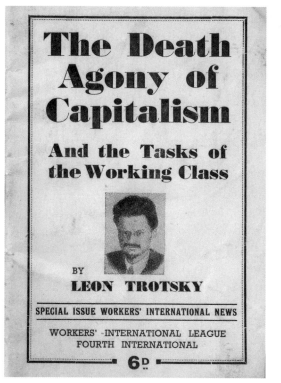

proclaim the new International? 'The Fourth International, we answer, has no need of being "proclaimed." It exists and it fights. It is weak? Yes, its ranks are not numerous because it is still young. They are as yet chiefly cadres. But these cadres are pledges for the future.' A crucial reality emphasized by the document from beginning to end was that the dominant organizational currents in the international working-class movement – Social-Democratic reformism and Stalinist authoritarianism – did not offer genuinely revolutionary perspectives that could lead to socialism. Nor could adequate leadership be provided by 'centrist' formations that pragmatically maintained a midway, compromised position between a revolutionary socialist orientation and the organizationally far more substantial battalions of Social Democracy and Stalinism. Only a revolutionary Marxist orientation was adequate for the tasks facing the world's working class and oppressed majorities. 'The advanced workers, united in the Fourth International, show their class the way out of the crisis. They offer a program based on international experience in the struggle of the proletariat and of all the oppressed of the world for liberation. They offer a spotless banner.'[35]

Peter Beilharz, an academic specializing in sociology and politics, has argued that 'Trotsky is at a loss to explain the "political backwardness" of the . . . working class' in the face of the capitalist crisis of the Great Depression, and that he therefore falls back on 'the factor of bad leadership . . . as *de facto* explanation for the situation.' Beilharz elaborates:

> Trotsky's response to the problem of [the lack of revolutionary] mass consciousness consists, therefore, in the presentation of a *Program*. For Trotsky a correct program – one corresponding to the objective situation – must override the immediate empirical consciousness of the proletariat. Those who know – the vanguard of the Fourth International – determine the real nature of the objective situation in order to bring the consciousness of the masses into conformity with it. Trotsky's dual error consists in a misreading of objective 'ripeness' [that is, the seeming inability of capitalism to get out of the multi-faceted crisis of the Great Depression without resort to authoritarianism and/or a horrific world war] coupled with the denial of the legitimacy of the masses' empirical consciousness. The response which calls for the 'Correct Program' avoids the real problems of everyday consciousness, instead turning the notion of transition into sloganizing and propaganda: as though when the masses hear the word, they will know how to act.[36]

A serious engagement with the text of the *Transitional Program* clearly indicates that it was historically specific, with primary reference points in the first third of the twentieth century (when Social Democratic reformism and Stalinism predominated in a relatively militant labour movement, for example) – in many ways vastly different from the landscape of the early twenty-first century. At the same time, Beilharz is right to identify a more universal element in the document, and also to declare that 'Trotsky's understanding of consciousness harks back to Marx.'[37] It could be added that Trotsky shares this understanding, as well, with others associated with the Marxist tradition in his time – including Rosa Luxemburg as well as Lenin and the majority current in the early Communist International. In this sense the much-vaunted *Transitional Program* contains nothing new.

The question is how to get from 'here' to 'there' – from the oppressive status quo of capitalism to the liberation of socialist revolution, from the current level of mass consciousness which accepts the capitalist status quo to a level of revolutionary consciousness determined to replace that with something better, and a practical strategic and tactical pathway capable of mobilizing enough workers to make it so. Yet Beilharz would be mistaken in assuming that Marx, Lenin, Luxemburg, Trotsky and the others believed that 'sloganizing and propaganda' would be sufficient in bringing about such change. Marx insisted that *only by going through a transformative process of actual struggle against capitalist oppression* could the working class develop the necessary revolutionary consciousness to make socialism a possibility. Luxemburg called for 'the daily struggle for reforms, for the amelioration of the condition of the workers within the framework of the existing social order, and for democratic institutions', concluding that for the Marxist movement, 'the struggle for reforms is its means; the social revolution, its aim.' Lenin similarly argued that 'the proletariat cannot be victorious except through democracy, i.e., by giving full effect to democracy and by linking with each step of its struggle democratic demands formulated in the most resolute terms.'[38]

This train of thought is what Trotsky attempts to drive home in the *Transitional Program*. 'It is necessary to help the masses in the process of the daily struggle to find the bridge between present demand and the socialist program of the revolution', he wrote. 'This bridge should include a system of *transitional demands*, stemming from today's conditions and from today's consciousness of wide layers of the working class and unalterably leading to one final conclusion: the conquest of power by the proletariat.' Involving increasing numbers of people in actual mass struggles, in the here and now, for goals that seem quite reasonable to them but which come into sharp collision with the capitalist status quo – this is what helps to generate revolutionary consciousness and revolutionary struggle.[39]

'How to mobilize the greatest possible numbers; how to raise the level of consciousness through action; how to create the most effective alliance of forces for the inescapable confrontation with the ruling classes' – this was the problematic with which Trotsky wrestled in this foundational document of the Fourth International. More than six decades after its founding, Fourth Internationalist Daniel Bensaïd emphasized his own understanding of the *Transitional Program*: 'The concept of transitional demands overcomes sterile antinomies between a reformist gradualism which believes in changing society without revolutionizing it, and a fetishism of the "glorious day" which reduces revolution to its climactic moment, to the detriment of the patient work of organization and education.'[40]

The founding document of the Fourth International in 1938 concluded: 'Workers – men and women – of all countries, place yourselves under the banner of the Fourth International. It is the banner of your approaching victory!'[41]

History was to take a different turn.

5

The Jaws of Death

Pavel Sudoplatov and Leonid Eitingon worked with the care and efficiency of professionals. Stalin told them: 'money is no object'.[1]

Three teams crystallized, each involving veterans from the Spanish Civil War, in some cases personally recruited by Eitingon, who spoke fluent Spanish and had done GPU work there. One team, operating in California and Mexico, involved Iosif R. Grigulevich, who had played a role in the liquidation of dissident Spanish leftists in 1937–8.

This team helped oversee another, headed by the Mexican artist David Alfaro Siqueiros, who had also been in Spain with the International Brigades and now led a small group of Mexican miners and peasants connected with their country's Communist Party. This was to be the 'hit squad' to end Trotsky's life.

Operating autonomously was a third team headed by Eitingon himself, involving Spanish Communist Caridad Mercader del Río and her son Ramón Mercader, also a Communist and a veteran of the war. Handsome, clever, dedicated to the cause, he was very gradually to insinuate himself into the Trotsky household, securing information and providing back-up if and when needed.

Life Rhythms

'The elaborate flood lights lend the residence the appearance of a Hollywood movie theatre during a world premiere', commented a U.S. volunteer upon her arrival at the Trotsky residence in Coyoacán. 'But the sentry box on the roof, the high walls, the barred windows and doors, and the intricate alarm system sharply alter that impression.' The sense of a fortress was enhanced by sentry booths on either side of the entrance, manned by well-armed Mexican police. 'A second line of defense is provided by inside guards who patrol the grounds within', backed up by a 'well-armed secretarial staff' inside the house.[2]

'In addition to the day's chores and seeing to security', recalled Bernard Wolfe, 'we, the members of the secretariat, kept a rotating guard shift through the night. There were three of us, a Frenchman, a Czech, and myself. That meant we split the night into three watches, early, middle, and late.' Every third night, Wolfe had to stay awake from midnight to dawn – and to keep himself awake, he got into the habit of, over and over again, taking apart and putting back together the Luger that he had been issued. 'Once, very late, the Old Man came through the dining room on his way to the bathroom, and saw me with parts of the gun in my hands and more parts spread on the table.' Wolfe and many of the other comrades often referred to Trotsky, with respectful affection, as 'the Old Man'.

> His hands-off style wouldn't allow him any tone of chiding or lecture. He just said quietly and seriously, 'You know, in the Revolution we lost more people than the enemy could claim credit for. Many young comrades killed themselves with their own guns and suicide was very far from their minds.'

Wolfe calmly responded: 'You don't have to worry about me, LD, I always take the clip out and make sure the chamber's empty, there's no danger here.' Another reason there was no danger, Wolfe confessed to readers of his memoir many years later, was that a spring from the gun's firing mechanism had flown out of the partially dismantled gun several minutes earlier. Despite considerable searching after Trotsky returned to bed, and for many nights before completing his stint in Mexico, Wolfe could never find that spring. 'The Luger was never to be fired again.'[3]

Sometimes u.s. guards and secretaries, along with Trotsky and Natalia, would make a surprise visit to the nearby modest home of Comrade Octavio Fernández and his family, which invariably would result in a festive party with alcoholic fruit drinks (*pulque*) and beer, music and dancing. 'The young girls, Graciela and Ofelia, exceptionally lithe and beautiful, and like the rest of the family superb dancers, pressed the guards, who were inclined to awkwardness, to join them in Mexican folk dancing', recalled Joe Hansen. 'If the guards did not know how, it was easy to learn! Trotsky took the side of the girls in putting on the pressure, although neither he nor Natalia attempted to join in. Dancing was for the young ones. As was the *pulque*. And the beer.'[4]

On occasion festivities would move to the Casa Azul. Diego Rivera and Frida Kahlo orchestrated an elaborate celebration of the twentieth anniversary of the Bolshevik Revolution (coinciding with Trotsky's birthday). Trotsky and Natalia were awakened by the serenades of a marimba band outside their bedroom window. There were many flowers and a large cake. The house and patio were filled, during the day-long fiesta, mostly with poor workers who were members of unions in which Trotsky's Mexican comrades were active. 'They brought food as gifts, including a few live chickens, their feet tied', and food and drink were shared generously. Although hesitant, Trotsky agreed to make a speech. 'It was a simple speech of thanks and appreciation. A few words about the October Revolution and its meaning. An expression of gratitude for the hospitality of Mexico and the warmth of the Mexican people . . . The audience responded with emotion and acclaim.'[5]

The work routines of the household, however, remained rigorous. Trotsky could be a severe taskmaster. 'Life quickly became miserable for anyone around Trotsky who found it difficult to break bohemian habits', recalled Hansen, 'or who found it insurmountably difficult to learn preciseness, thoroughness, workmanship.'[6]

Yet there was humour to be found in difficult circumstances. Even the Moscow Trials 'did not lack a humorous angle', according to Rae Spiegel. 'The chimerical accusation that Trotsky earned a million dollars as an "agent of Hitler" seemed like a monstrous joke at the expense of this household that is perennially "broke."' The simplest food items sometimes were beyond the boundaries of the household budget – 'we were forced to cut eggs and butter from our breakfast menu and meat from our dinner.' Playing off this reality and the accusation of abundant Hitlerite money, Spiegel jokingly 'demanded' eggs and buttered toast for breakfast. Spiegel notes that 'LD himself was completely unaware of his material surroundings', although before long, he would secure chickens and rabbits to raise, and add to his household routine the tasks of tending them and seeing to small-scale gardening. On the other hand, when he overheard Spiegel and Natalia plotting to buy him a more comfortable chair, he strenuously objected to such 'luxury', adding that hard chairs 'were best for working'.[7]

There were excursions, nonetheless – periodic drives into the country for picnics, an occasional fishing expedition in Veracruz and seeking out various types of Mexican cactus, which the intrigued Trotsky would carefully dig up and bring back for replanting in Coyoacán.

The Horrific Storm

In 1939, concluding that the People's Front strategy had proved incapable of stopping fascism and war, with the 'capitalist democracies' hesitant to make an alliance with the USSR, the Stalin regime decided to sign a non-aggression pact with Nazi Germany. As Trotsky noted, 'Stalin's alliance with Hitler raised the curtain on the world war and led directly to the enslavement of the Polish people', and 'Germany has now unloosed all the furies of hell in a major offensive to which the Allies are replying in kind with all their forces of destruction. From now on the life of Europe and all of mankind will be determined for a long time by the course of the imperialist war and by its economic and political consequences.'[8] Trotsky saw the Second World War as containing the same kinds of dynamics that had brought the first great war of imperialist slaughter. But he saw more than this. Trotsky 'emphasized the necessity of conceiving a fact not merely as something which exists, but also as something which is in the process of becoming', novelist James T. Farrell once commented. 'This sense of becoming in events, of the relational character of events to each other was one of his most remarkable traits . . . He never isolated political events; he saw them constantly in their international setting . . . '.[9]

In 1937 Trotsky had offered a number of insightful predictions about what he viewed as an inevitable Second World War. 'The next war will have a totalitarian character, not only in the sense that its operations will develop simultaneously on the earth, under the earth, on the water, under the water, in the air, including the stratosphere', he wrote, 'but also in the sense that it will draw into its vortex the whole population, all its material as well as spiritual riches.' He predicted that, given its 'geographical location, territorial dimensions, size of population, resources of war materials, reserves of gold and technology . . . domination over our planet will fall to the lot of the United States'. On the other hand, the British Empire and other colonial empires would not endure – the war would generate 'frictions, antagonisms, and centrifugal tendencies' which sooner or later would 'find their expression in insurrections and revolution'. This war would be far more destructive than the last – 'the extermination of human lives and the expenditure of war materials will, from the very beginning, be several times greater than at the beginning of the last war, and will at the same time have a tendency to further rapid increase. The tempos will be more feverish, the destructive forces more grandiose, the distress of the population more unbearable.' On one point the optimistic wish overpowered the pitiless analysis: 'A political revolution in the USSR – that is, the overthrow of the bureaucratic caste, which is decomposed to the very marrow – will undoubtedly be one of the first results of the war.' On the other hand, his take on the future of the German and Italian war efforts posited that 'if at the beginning of the war these states may and do score imposing military successes, then in the second stage they will become the arena of social convulsions earlier than their enemies.' He concluded: 'Not a single country will escape the consequences of the war. In pains and convulsions the whole world will change its face.'[10]

Trotsky's thoughts of 1937 on the role of the USSR in the war are worth lingering over. 'The current contemptuous appraisal of the Red Army is just as one-sided as yesterday's belief in the indestructibility of Stalin's domination', he argued. 'The frame-up and execution of the idols of yesterday naturally induce doubt and demoralization in the ranks of the army. Nevertheless, the displays and maneuvers which demonstrate to the foreign generals the endurance, mobility, and ingenuity of the Soviet soldier and officer remain a reality, together with the high qualities of the Soviet tanks and airplanes, the audacity and skill of the Soviet fliers.' In Trotsky's view this bore witness 'to the tremendous economic and cultural growth of the country, which reconciles itself with ever-increasing difficulty to Stalin's regime.' He saw this as the positive result of the Revolution of 1917, and added: 'If humanity itself is not hurled into barbarism, the social bases of the Soviet regime (new forms of property and planned economy) will resist the test of war and even be reinforced.' In regard to the military dimensions of the coming war, he suggested that Hitler's war machine on the Eastern Front might be brought to 'complete collapse' at the hands of 'Russia's strong navy and air force' combined with '"the moral factor", that is, the living people: the Red soldier, worker, peasant'.[11]

In his analysis *The Meaning of the Second World War*, Ernest Mandel (attempting to further develop Trotsky's approach) would later note that the destructiveness of the conflict was what Trotsky had predicted. 'The legacy of destruction left by World War II is staggering. Eighty million people were killed, if one includes those who died of starvation and illness as a result of the war – eight times as many as during World War I', Mandel noted. 'Dozens of cities were virtually totally destroyed, especially in Japan and Germany. Material resources capable of feeding, clothing, housing, equipping all the poor of this world were wasted for purely destructive purposes. Forests were torn down and agricultural land converted into wasteland on a scale not witnessed since the Thirty Years War or the Mongol invasion of the Islamic Empire.'[12]

According to Mandel, the Second World War 'must be grasped as five different conflicts'. There was, first of all, an inter-imperialist war fought for global hegemony – particularly for raw materials, markets and investment opportunities. There was, second, a war of self-defence waged by the Soviet Union against an imperialist attempt to colonize the country. Third, there was a war of the Chinese people against imperialist invasion, accompanied – at certain points – by a civil war between Chinese Nationalists and Chinese Communists. Fourth, there was a war of Asian colonial peoples for independence against various foreign oppressors and aggressors. Fifth was a war of national liberation fought by populations of the occupied countries of Europe.[13]

Yet the Hitler-Stalin pact of 1939 now caused many to see an essential 'totalitarian' identity of Nazi Germany and Stalinist Russia, confirmed by the 'Soviet imperialism' of the USSR's taking over of new territories (specified by secret codicils of the pact): eastern Poland, Latvia, Lithuania and Estonia, and an invasion of Finland to boot! Trotsky was critical of these violations of national sovereignty, but he also saw them as nothing more than defensive tactical moves (which even had a 'progressive' dimension, given the overturn of capitalist property relations in the Soviet-conquered territories). He insisted that the USSR was fighting a defensive war, in contrast to Germany's 'aggressive' war, and that the Marxist understanding of imperialism is grounded in what Marx called the *capital accumulation process*, which was non-existent in the Soviet Union. He predicted that the German-Soviet pact would not last long – that Hitler would soon launch an invasion of the USSR. He also continued to insist that the USSR was a 'degenerated workers' state'. Its progressive, post-capitalist property relations (nationalized and planned economy) must be defended by a democratizing political revolution to overthrow Stalin's regime, but it must also be defended in any confrontation with capitalist powers. Many in the Fourth International sharply disagreed, arguing that the USSR was in no way a 'workers' state' but represented either 'state capitalism' or a new form of class society, 'bureaucratic collectivism' – in either case, it was no better than Germany or the United States, and not worthy of defence.[14]

A number of Trotsky's adherents were beginning to follow some left-wing intellectuals around the world in their abandonment of Marxist perspectives.[15] Others sought to harmonize their new perspectives with revolutionary Marxism, but multiple fractures and fissures began to open up in the world Trotskyist movement. Many comrades rallied to Trotsky's efforts to hold together a

Fourth International capable of providing effective revolutionary leadership in the face of difficult times and future opportunities. But a succession of splits were in the offing as the Second World War unfolded.

What Was, What Is, What Might Be

Trotsky had mixed feelings about writing a biography of Stalin, an undertaking largely inspired by a contract offered from a major publishing house, with substantial advance payment that would help the Coyoacán household to meet its expenses. His young aide Joseph Hansen argued that 'he could use Stalin as a foil for putting the record straight about the history of the Bolshevik party and that this was very important for the generation I belonged to.'[16] This became an essential element in Trotsky's composition of the biography. The book has a richness similar to the fact-filled work by his former comrade Boris Souvarine, *Stalin: A Critical Survey of Bolshevism*, a work Trotsky praised as a source of information but condemned for presenting Stalinism as rising out of flaws inherent in Bolshevism.[17]

Trotsky defended the conception of *professional revolutionary* from Sourvarine's critique, emphasizing the freshness and idealism of the revolutionary activists who organized to overthrow monarchy and capitalism in the Russian empire. 'The youth of the revolutionary generation coincided with the youth of the labor movement', he recalled. 'It was the epoch of people between the ages of eighteen and thirty. Revolutionists above that age were few in number and seemed old men.' He remembered a movement 'as yet utterly devoid of careerism', living on 'its faith in the future and on its spirit of self-sacrifice'. He also recalled a poignant innocence: 'There were as yet no routines, no set formulae, no theatrical gestures, no ready-made oratorical tricks. The struggle was by nature full of pathos, shy and awkward.' This blended with deep commitments:

> Whoever joined an organization knew that prison followed
> by exile awaited him within the next few months. The measure
> of ambition was to last as long as possible on the job prior to
> arrest; to hold oneself steadfast when facing the gendarmes;
> to ease, as far as possible, the plight of one's comrades; to read,
> while in prison, as many books as possible; to escape as soon
> as possible from exile abroad; to acquire wisdom there; and
> then return to revolutionary activity in Russia.

Such 'professional revolutionists believed what they taught. . . . Solidarity under persecution was no empty word, and it was augmented by contempt for cowardice and desertion.' Trotsky recalled the description of the activists in the Odessa underground of 1901–7 offered by Eugenia Levitskaya: 'Turning over in my mind the mass of comrades with whom I had occasion to meet', she had reminisced, 'I cannot recall a single reprehensible, contemptible act, a single deception or lie.' To be sure, friction and factional differences were in evidence, 'but no more than that. Somehow everyone looked after himself morally, became better and more gentle in that friendly family.' It is striking that Trotsky would focus on such gentleness and devotion, stressing that this was not the exception but the rule. 'The young men and young women who devoted themselves entirely to the revolutionary movement, without demanding anything in return, were not the worst representatives of their generation', he insisted. 'The order of "professional revolutionists" cannot suffer by comparison with any other social group.'[18]

The basic logic of Lenin's organizational approach was emphasized as Trotsky described his own anti-Lenin position in the years before 1917:

My position on the intra-party conflict came down to this: as long as the revolutionary intellectuals were dominant among the Bolsheviks as well as among the Mensheviks and as long as both factions did not venture beyond the bourgeois democratic revolution, there was no justification for a split between them; in the new revolution, under the pressure of the laboring masses, both factions would in any case he compelled to assume an identical revolutionary position, as they did in 1905.

While many latter-day activists were attracted to his 'old conciliationism as the voice of wisdom', Trotsky now insisted that its 'profound erroneousness' had been proved in both theory and practice: 'A simple conciliation of factions is possible only along some sort of "middle" line', he noted. 'But where is the guarantee that this artificially drawn diagonal line will coincide with the needs of objective development? The task of scientific politics is to deduce a program and a tactic from an analysis of the struggle of classes, not from the parallelogram of such secondary and transitory forces as political factions.' He insisted that a revolutionary party would be unable to train its cadres without such 'scientific politics', concluding:

> The policy of conciliation thrived on the hope that the course of events itself would prompt the necessary tactic. But that fatalistic optimism meant in practice not only repudiation of factional struggle but of the very idea of a party, because, if 'the course of events' is capable of directly dictating to the masses the correct policy, what is the use of any special unification of the proletarian vanguard, the working out of a program, the choice of leaders, the training in a spirit of discipline?[19]

Another aspect of Trotsky's efforts involved combating 'the drift of the anti-Stalinist intellectuals from Marxism towards reformism', to quote two of Trotsky's u.s. comrades, James Burnham and Max Shachtman, in their lengthy and brilliant critical survey 'Intellectuals in Retreat', which appeared in the theoretical journal *New International* in January 1939. Ironically, while he noted of the Burnham-Shachtman article that 'many parts are excellent', it contained passages that were dismissive aspects of Marxism's dialectical philosophy, reflecting the broader trend of scepticism towards revolutionary Marxism about which Trotsky was deeply concerned. (Before long, they would lead a major oppositional struggle against him in the Fourth International, with Burnham soon abandoning Marxism altogether and becoming an influential political conservative.) The undertow of de-radicalization among the once leftward-moving intellectuals, with proliferating questions about Marxism and a growing rejection of the Bolshevik-Leninist tradition, was particularly upsetting to him.[20] He lashed out at all tendencies that he perceived as going in that direction, including among such outstanding comrades as Victor Serge – to the point of excess, many have concluded. On the other hand, a serious examination of the recently published edition of Serge's eloquent memoirs, restoring portions that were previously cut, indicate that some of Serge's thinking contained precisely the kind of fundamental questioning of the tradition that so deeply concerned Trotsky:

Bolshevik thought draws its inspiration from the feeling of possession of the truth. In the eyes of Lenin . . . dialectical materialism is both the law of human thought as well as that of the development of nature and of societies. Bolshevik thinking is grounded in the possession of the truth. The Party is the repository of the truth, and any form of thinking that differs from it is a dangerous or reactionary error. Here lies the spiritual source of its intolerance. The absolute conviction of its lofty mission assures it of a moral energy quite astonishing in its intensity – and, at the same time, a clerical mentality which is quick to become Inquisitorial. Lenin's 'proletarian Jacobinism', with its detachment and discipline both in thought and action, is eventually molded by the old regime, that is, by the struggle against despotism. I am quite convinced that a sort of natural selection of authoritarian temperaments is the result. Finally, the victory of the revolution deals with the inferiority complex of the perpetually bullied masses by arousing in them a spirit of social revenge, which in turn tends to generate new despotic institutions. I was witness to the great intoxication with which yesterday's sailors and workers exercised command and enjoyed the satisfaction of demonstrating that they were now in power![21]

Pushing hard against the demoralization of those who seemed to be distancing themselves from the revolutionary struggle, Trotsky's revolutionary internationalism became more strident: 'Let the disillusioned ones bury their own dead. The working class is not a corpse. As hitherto, our society rests upon it. It needs a new leadership. It will find this nowhere but in the Fourth International. All that is rational is real. Social Democracy and Stalinocracy even today represent stupendous fictions. But the Fourth International is an impregnable reality.'[22]

Trotsky insisted on the purity of the earlier generation of revolutionaries (to which he had belonged), as well as on the logic of the Leninist conception of organization (to which he had been won). And he had always defended the purity of the socialist goal against Stalinism:

Socialism signifies a pure and clear social system which is accommodated to the self-government of the toilers. Stalin's regime is based on a conspiracy of the rulers against the ruled. Socialism implies an uninterrupted growth of universal equality. Stalin has erected a system of revolting privileges.

Socialism has as its goal the all-sided flowering of the individual personality. When and where has man's personality been so degraded as in the USSR?

Socialism would have no value apart from unselfish, honest, and humane relations between human beings. The Stalin regime has permeated social and personal relationships with lies, careerism, and treachery.[23]

One can get a sense of Trotsky's situation by considering his interactions with the three most famous muralists among Mexico's revolutionary artists – Diego Rivera, José Clemente Orozco and David Alfaro Siqueiros.

'Rivera is one of those monsters of fecundity such as occur but rarely in the history of mankind', wrote Bertram D. Wolfe (not to be confused with the Trotskyist Bernard Wolfe) in a biography of 1939. 'Such men enlarge our faith in the capabilities of man.' Wolfe compared the 'universality of this love of life' to the American poet Walt Whitman, saying that Rivera had 'a like love of man and appetite for life' and noting that Rivera's 'paintings on the walls of Mexico's public buildings are one, long, beguiling fable concerning his world, his time, his country, its past, its present, its future'.[24]

Trotsky was especially close to Rivera personally, but the two strong and vibrant personalities sometimes grated against each other. A politically disillusioned Wolfe, in a later study of Rivera, makes flippant reference to 'his Trotskyism, which no one, Diego least of all, had taken seriously' (thereby presenting him, Dora Apel tartly notes, as 'a political clown'), and Wolfe offers this account of the break between the two men: 'When Trotsky was his honored guest, he drove the old man into such a towering rage by outrageous inventions of "facts" and doctrines in the field of politics that the argument ended with Trotsky and his wife packing their bags and leaving their goods on the sidewalk until they could find new refuge.'[25]

Wolfe's latter-day assertions obscure more than they reveal. While some questioned how deep Rivera's 'Trotskyism' went (he himself confessed to having an anarchist streak), there is little indication that his commitment to the Trotskyist movement was not serious. When Jean van Heijenoort expressed scepticism about the political stability of the warm and generous but sometimes volatile Rivera, 'Trotsky told me, not without a tone of reproach, "Diego, you know, is a revolutionary!"' By all accounts, Trotsky enjoyed talking with Rivera and spent much time with him – 'Rivera was the only person who could come to the house at any time without previous arrangement, and Trotsky always received him warmly', according to Van Heijenoort. The rift, which Trotsky sought to avoid, was more drawn out than Wolfe suggests, with an escalating series of grievances culminating in Rivera publicly supporting a maverick 'bourgeois' political candidate, which meant a final break from the Trotskyist movement. There was about a month from the time of the break to the time when the Trotsky household moved to a new location, Avenida Viena, in March 1939. Even then, 'I don't think that Trotsky's personal regard for Rivera was changed in the least', recalled Joseph Hansen. 'His admiration and appreciation remained and he still talked about him as if their friendship had not been affected.'[26]

Orozco's work is much darker than Rivera's, and Trotsky's connection with him was far more limited, yet this had a significance of its own. 'Mourning and death were recurrent themes in the work of Orozco', according to Ralph E. Shikes, displaying 'the bitterest memories' and 'a sensitivity to human suffering . . . [that was] passionate in outlook and dynamic in handling'. Trotsky went out of his way to connect with Orozco. Van Heijenoort noted that Orozco and Rivera, 'in tastes, ways of life, and styles of painting . . . were at opposite poles', adding that 'Orozco was as tormented an introvert as Rivera was a hearty extrovert.' The unrelieved tragedy, violence, betrayal and corruption depicted in Orozco's work – more than Rivera's purposeful historical frescoes, with their life-affirming optimism – seemed to capture aspects of a reality that was all too prevalent in Trotsky's experience, and the global experience, during the years of his final exile. Upon leaving the artist's studio, Trotsky exclaimed, 'He is a Dostoevsky!'[27]

What, then, is Siqueiros? However one tries to answer this question artistically, politically he was an agent of Stalin, committed to murdering Leon Trotsky. Dressed as Mexican policemen, he and his team overpowered and tied up the actual policemen and were then given entry to the compound by the guard on duty, Sheldon Harte, who seems to have been a naive young radical with Stalinist sympathies posing as a Trotskyist. Trotsky's grandson Seva, many years later, recounted:

From three sides they attacked Trotsky and Natalia's bedroom with Thompson machineguns. Thanks to her sharp reflexes, Natalia quickly pushed the Old Man off the bed and shielded him in a dark corner of the bedroom. Those reflexes saved both of their lives that day.

At the time I slept in the adjacent bedroom, and during the attack a bullet grazed the big toe of my left foot. The attackers launched incendiary grenades into my bedroom in an effort to set aflame the room where Trotsky's extensive archives were kept, this effort that was Stalin's calling card as only he would be so interested in erasing those files.[28]

As Trotsky emerged from his bullet-riddled room, 'his hair was ruffled, kind of flying in the wind', recalled one of his guards, Jake Cooper. 'He looked amazingly calm considering what he had just gone through. I thought to myself that Trotsky had probably gone through situations as bad or worse during the Russian Revolution, such that this situation didn't really shake him.' Amazingly no one was killed, but Sheldon Harte was missing. He was taken with the Siqueiros team to their hideaway. Harte was frightened and indignant, apparently having been led to believe that no one would be harmed, that the Siqueiros group was simply after Trotsky's papers. Under the circumstances it was deemed necessary to kill Harte and bury him under the floor, covered in quicklime.[29]

After the attack, his grandson reports, Trotsky would say as he awoke each morning: 'Natasha, they have given us another day to live.' He had almost three more months, while Leonid Eitingon's fallback plan was put into effect.

'Success'

Imagine the filth of the 'special task'. Vitorio Vidali – a dedicated Italian Communist serving under the name 'Contreras' as the heroic commander of an International Brigade in Spain– would recall a highly placed comrade from the USSR (a Comintern or GPU official?) telling him: 'We must be very, very wily. . . . Don't forget that word even in the most difficult moments. We must be open-minded and wily.' Vidali was in Mexico, some have said, to assist in the assassination of Leon Trotsky. Whether or not that is true, upon reflection, Vidali connected this 'wily' advice with 'a "theory" concerning the "usefulness" of people, of the masses', positing that 'even a movement can be considered useful or useless. As long as it remains useful, it is utilized; when it no longer serves its purpose it is rejected, or suffocated, or destroyed.' And he recalled, 'I stood there with a nasty taste in my mouth.'[30]

Imagine one who glories in being wily – in the name of the highest ideals of humanity he manipulates the ideals and desires of another person, utilizes her desires in order to destroy someone who is the personification of her ideals. Uses a person, 'makes love' to her over and over, pretends to care about her, weaves together a phony relationship over time, simply to secure information for her enemies,

Ramón Mercader.

and, with his own hand, destroys her hero. Helps some good people in order to move closer to killing their friend. Gives a toy to a child for the purpose of positioning himself to murder his grandfather.

The details have been elaborated and documented elsewhere.[31] GPU agent Ramón Mercader, using false identities and aliases (Jacques Mornard, Frank Jacson), was able to pass himself off as a wealthy and charming Belgian playboy with vague business connections but who was beginning to look for meaning in life – a relationship with a down-to-earth woman, an engagement with politics that could bring a better world. He won his way into the heart of an idealistic young revolutionary from the United States, Sylvia Ageloff, who happened to be a Trotskyist and in a position to serve as a secretary in the Trotsky household. In a gradual, subtle, wily manner, 'Frank Jacson' was able to maneouvre himself – presumably as someone being drawn into the Trotskyist movement – into a position to have a one-on-one discussion with Trotsky, in his study.

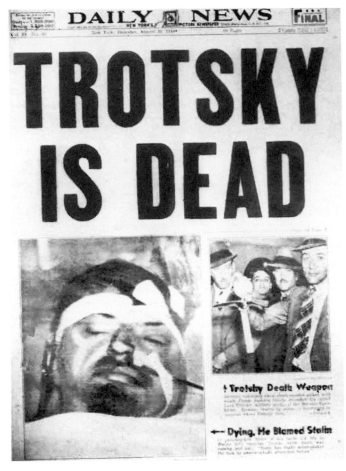

Trotsky's death announced in *The Daily News*.

Trotsky's scream was bloodcurdling – and Natalia as well as some of the guards and secretaries came running to see Trotsky covered in blood from a head wound made by an alpine axe, struggling with the assassin. Mercader, restrained by the guards, was being brutally beaten. 'Tell the boys not to kill him', Trotsky, now in Natalia's arms, said to Hansen. 'He must be made to talk.' Trotsky's fourteen-year-old grandson, just returned from school, stood in the doorway, recalling years later:

It still seems as if it were yesterday when I looked through the half open door to the library and saw my grandfather fatally wounded, lying on the floor, his forehead bloodied, and by his side his inseparable companion Natalia, applying ice to his wound, trying to stem the bleeding. And also there beside him, as best I recall, were the u.s. comrades Charley Cornell and Joe Hansen. When Trotsky heard me approach from the next room he struggled to say, 'keep Seva out, he shouldn't see this.'[32]

Disoriented yet in some ways still cogent, Trotsky said, 'I feel . . . here', he pointed to his heart, 'this is the end . . . this time they've succeeded.' An ambulance came, bringing him to the hospital. Natalia was with him. She later recalled:

The nurses began to cut his clothes. Suddenly he said to me distinctly but very sadly and gravely, 'I don't want them to undress me . . . I want you to do it . . .' These were his last words to me. I undressed him, and pressed my lips to his. He returned the kiss once, twice and again. Then he lost consciousness.[33]

6

Afterlife

The medical staff at the Cruz Verde hospital did their best to repair what the assassin had done. 'I watched over him all that night, waiting for the "awakening"', Natalia later recounted. 'The eyes were closed, but the breathing, now heavy, now even and calm, inspired hope.' A day passed, but 'the wound had penetrated the brain too deeply. The awakening, so passionately awaited, never came.' Trotsky died 25 hours after the attack. The following day his body was taken to the Alcazar Funeral Home.[1]

On 22 August a funeral cortege gathered. When a black-veiled Natalia emerged after some last private moments with her companion, the crowds called out 'Trotsky lives! Viva Trotsky! Death to Stalin!' Trotsky's casket, covered with the red flag of revolution and flowers, was followed by Joe Hansen, Otto Schüssler and the other guards, as well as members of Trotsky's household. A number of dignitaries were also on hand, and large crowds consisting largely of the labouring poor. Lillian Pollak noted:

> These people know Trotsky although they have not met him. They know his story, because Mexico's past is full of revolutionary martyrs. Trotsky is the brave revolutionist who fought for the dispossessed, the oppressed. They know him as a man with simple tastes who gathered cactus in the countryside and tended rabbits in his garden. They have heard he was a world-famous leader, an orator, a fine writer,

who fought for truth and humanity with his pen and they
know that although he made errors in his life-time, he never
swerved in his fight for truth, for humanity, for socialism,
and for that he was killed.[2]

They walked eight miles, and at the conclusion tribute was
paid in brief speeches by Albert Goldman, the lawyer at the Dewey
hearings, Garcia Trevino, a well-known trade union leader and
socialist, and Spanish Trotskyist Grandizo Munis, who repeated
Trotsky's parting words: 'Estoy seguro de la Victoria de la Cuarta
International. Adelante.'[3]

Trotsky's body lay in state for five days, with 100,000 people
coming to pay respects, according to Charles Cornell, a mingling
of 'dark-skinned Indian women carrying babies in their shawls',
campesinos 'in their white outfits and bright serapes', well-dressed
intellectuals, students from the universities, and urban workers
with 'the soil of a day's work still on their knotty hands and blue
overalls'. In the streets, some sang a freshly composed ballad
(a *corrido*, typically created to lament the death and celebrate the
life of a popular figure), telling Trotsky's story:

Stalin and the assassin
in frank cooperation
carried their crime with precision
to its final destination.
Expelled from his country
He wandered through many nations
always fighting bitterly
to combat oppression.[4]

Trotsky's 'revenge' against the man who had him killed is
reflected in the time leading up to the death of each. 'Full of
calamity and sorrow as Trotsky's last years were, they were not

without the solace of love and of comradeship in a common struggle or without the satisfactions wrested from that struggle', scholar Paul Siegel notes, 'while the last years of Stalin, who had the power to minister to all his desires, were utterly desolate.' The dictator's view of himself, his comrades, and the future is suggested in his late-in-life outburst at a Political Bureau meeting of the Communist Party of the Soviet Union: 'You are blind like young kittens; what will happen without me? The country will perish because you do not know how to recognize enemies.' His victim of 1940 had a different sense of things.[5]

Not long before his death, Trotsky penned what has been termed his 'testament'. Beginning with the anticipation of a 'betrayal' by his own body (reflected in high and rising blood pressure), the possibility that his death might be perpetrated by the Communist movement's infamous betrayer is suggested by his denunciation of the Stalin regime. The remainder of the brief document interweaves tender feelings toward his companion Natalia Sedova with revolutionary Marxist commitments, culminating in hopeful words about what future generations may realize: 'Natasha has just come up to the window from the courtyard and opened it wider so that the air may enter more freely into my room. I can see the bright green strip of grass beneath the wall, and the clear blue sky above the wall, and sunlight everywhere. Life is beautiful. Let the future generations cleanse it of all evil, oppression, and violence and enjoy it to the full.'[6]

What Happened Next

'I am confident in the victory of the Fourth International. Go forward!' These were the last words Trotsky spoke to Joseph Hansen. In helping to found this 'world party of socialist revolution', Trotsky had predicted that the coming Second World War would generate an even greater wave of militant working-class insurgency than had been the case with the First World War. Working-class revolutions would sweep away Stalinism in the USSR and would also break the power of the capitalists in the advanced industrial countries. 'The new generation of workers whom the war will impel onto the road of revolution will take their place under our banner', he asserted on the eve of his death.[7] Handfuls of activists throughout the world rallied to that banner, to end all forms of human oppression and degradation, to create a cooperative commonwealth in which the free development of each would be the condition for the free development of all. Yet fascism, Stalinism, imperialism and war were engulfing the world, and many comrades were destroyed in the high tide of authoritarianism and violence.

There *were* revolutionary upsurges throughout the colonial and semi-colonial countries of Asia, Africa and Latin America. But Stalinism took on renewed life in the post-war period. It seemed as solid as ever in the USSR, gaining immense authority through the 'Great Patriotic War' which drove back and destroyed the Nazi aggressor. Communist parties had played central roles in popular resistance movements throughout the world, from France and Italy to China and Vietnam. Stalinism also took advantage of radical ferment in Eastern Europe – and of a cynical 'spheres of influence' understanding with the governments of Britain and the United States – to establish its hold on this area, setting up Communist Party dictatorships loyal to the USSR to form a buffer zone between the USSR and its erstwhile wartime allies of the capitalist West. Outside the buffer zone, Yugoslav and Greek Communist partisans, with much popular support – but without Stalin's – sought to carry out revolutions, successfully in the first case. China and Vietnam also more or less went the way of Yugoslavia. In France and Italy Communist-led resistance movements, more obedient to Stalin, held back from revolutionary attempts. Still, in the capitalist countries of Western Europe masses of workers flocked not to the handfuls of stalwart Trotskyists, but to the already existing Communist, Social Democratic and Labour parties.[8]

A now quite powerful United States of America established the Marshall Plan to rebuild the economies of Western Europe on a firm capitalist basis. A North Atlantic Treaty Organization was fashioned to prevent the Soviet Red Army from expanding further westward, but also – and no less important – to prevent indigenous revolutionaries from replacing weakened bourgeois regimes with new workers' republics. The reformist Social Democratic and Labour parties forged a firm alliance with what was left of their own capitalist classes, and with the United States, as the Cold War set in. The world seemed divided between capitalist and 'Communist' superpowers: the 'Free World' bloc (including both capitalist republics and right-wing dictatorships) led by the u.s. versus the 'Iron Curtain' countries (with bureaucratic dictatorships but collectivized economies) led by the ussr.

Stalinist parties claimed to represent working-class interests. Countries they ruled over experienced policies of modernization and full employment. Co-existing uneasily with the stranglehold of bureaucratic tyranny was the expansion of education, healthcare, housing and other social services beneficial to those who laboured.

Economically advanced capitalist countries saw efforts at expanding prosperity to benefit all classes in the post-Second World War period, to win hearts and minds of labouring masses who might otherwise be attracted to Communism. Government and business policies fostered 'higher wages, shorter working hours, paid holidays, full employment and the virtual disappearance of unemployment, construction of wholesome and cheap housing, social security protection against sickness, loss of work, and old age'.[9] The dramatic development of the welfare state after 1945 – in large measure won through the pressure of labour movements led by Social Democratic and Labour parties – was more or less

A modest monument marks the site of Trotsky's and Natalia's ashes, located on the grounds of their final home together, now the Leon Trotsky Museum. (Natalia moved from Coyoacán to Paris in 1960, and died in 1962.)

supported by conservative parties as well, under the pressure of the Cold War power struggle.

The working classes of Western Europe and North America – despite ongoing discontents and periodic troubles that could generate militant struggles – experienced sufficiently improved living conditions and tentatively hopeful expectations that more generally tended to block the revolutionary upsurges that Trotsky had anticipated.

Yet anti-imperialist and anti-colonial insurgencies in the 'third world' countries of Asia, Africa and Latin America fulfilled many of Trotsky's expectations. Some of the struggles were led by Stalinist parties, however, and with victory they became part of the Communist Bloc. When victorious struggles were led by

Trotsky and Natalia Sedova, 1940.

non-Communists, the newly independent countries clustered together in a somewhat equivocal, more or less left-nationalist Non-Aligned Bloc. A few (most notably Cuba) did not fit neatly into either. The revolutionary stirrings in the third world and the renewed power of Social Democratic and Labour parties in Western Europe (not to mention massive Communist parties in Italy and France) generated hopes in possibilities to move beyond capitalism. But this was largely overshadowed by the fact that world politics appeared to be locked into a grim 'superpower' confrontation that threatened to spiral into a new world war – an especially devastating prospect since both sides had developed nuclear weapons.[10]

This complex situation – combined with the obvious incorrectness of Trotsky's prediction regarding post-war realities – generated sharp controversies inside the Fourth International, fragmenting the world Trotskyist movement. Perry Anderson once commented that, nonetheless, this 'tradition – persecuted, reviled, isolated, divided – will have to be studied in all the diversity of its underground channels and streams', adding: 'It may surprise future historians with its resources.'[11]

As Marx had insisted, societies divided between oppressive minorities and oppressed majorities, exploiters and exploited, particularly given the growing complexities and voracious dynamism of global capitalism, inevitably generate revolutionary ferment and uprisings. From the 1960s to the '80s, a 'new left' generation of activists engaged with Trotsky's ideas and gave them new life – particularly as the crisis of Stalinism and its successors became increasingly evident, as capitalism seemed to be entering a long-term crisis of its own and as Social-Democratic reformism began to hit a dead end.[12]

Then the collapse of 'Communist' variants derived from the Stalinist experience meshed with neo-liberal onslaughts and the wonders of 'globalization'. None of this galvanized workers and revolutionaries into a force for which Trotsky's perspectives had obvious applications.[13] The revolutionary left largely succumbed to what might be called 'the Three Ds' – disorientation, disappointment, disintegration.

Trotsky biographer Irving Howe opined in the late 1970s: 'Despite Trotsky's grandiose predictions about the future of his Fourth International, Trotskyism as a political movement has for many years been without political or intellectual significance: a petrified ideology.' A more recent biographer, Joshua Rubenstein, also emphasizes Trotskyism's irrelevance. 'The Fourth International was never more than a ramshackle collection of orthodox Marxists', he tells us, with 'a history of quarreling among fewer and fewer people . . . as detached from reality as their hero had been at times in his life . . . He refused to renounce the revolution that first betrayed, then destroyed him. He could not renounce himself.'[14]

It was not the revolution, Trotsky would have said, but the Stalinist counter-revolution that was responsible for such betrayal and murder. And new crises continue to generate radical ferment. Since the 1980s, one might argue, Trotsky's influence – rather than simply evaporating – has been diffused within what remains of the radical left.

Legacy

Trotsky's perspectives are inseparable from those of Marx and Engels, Luxemburg, Lenin and others. Within the evolving Marxist tradition, different revolutionaries came to certain insights and clarifications before others. Various theorists also gave a distinctive articulation to certain ideas: Gramsci's discussion of 'hegemony' and Luxemburg's description of the 'mass strike', as well as Lenin's insights on the 'revolutionary party' and on the 'worker-peasant alliance', are a few of the examples that come to mind. Unlike the others, Trotsky lived as late as 1940, which enabled him to make certain contributions not allowed to them.[15] Defining features of Trotsky's thought might include:

(1) his development of the theory of uneven and combined development and the related theory of permanent revolution;
(2) his understanding of the Russian Revolution of 1917, reflected in his actions of that year and in his three-volume *History of the Russian Revolution*;
(3) his articulation (along with Lenin and others in the Communist International) of the united front tactic;
(4) his increasingly profound critique, from 1923 onward, of the bureaucratic degeneration within the Soviet Republic, of the authoritarianism that accompanied it, and his retrieval of the concept of 'workers' democracy' (including, finally, the principle of political pluralism) that had been central to the revolutionary struggles of 1905 and 1917;

(5) his defence of revolutionary internationalism against the notion of 'socialism in one country' – understanding that in the global political economy, the fates of the working classes and oppressed peoples of the early Soviet Union were interlinked with those of the 'advanced' capitalist countries and with those in the 'under-developed' colonial and semi-colonial regions;

(6) his analysis of the bureaucratic degeneration of the Soviet Union in *The Revolution Betrayed*, and his exposure of and opposition to the poisonous and murderous characteristics of Stalinism as reflected in the Moscow trials and massive repression in the Soviet Union in the late 1930s;

(7) his analysis of fascism and his urgent call for a working-class united front to combat and defeat it;

(8) his critique of the popular front as class-collaborationist with built-in dynamics of defeat;

(9) his analysis of the underlying dynamics of the Second World War, providing insights into post-war realities;

(10) his efforts to draw an international network of uncorrupted revolutionaries together into a Fourth International, armed with revolutionary Marxist perspectives, including a considerable amount of attention to questions of the creation and dynamics of revolutionary parties.

Trotsky, resistant to the conversion of all this into a dogmatic 'orthodoxy', dismissed efforts to devise a set of 'Trotskyist' tactics to be applied 'from Paris to Honolulu'. More than this, one might insist, there are serious limitations in some of what he had to say. This is something that historians can explore and debate – and, in a more important sense, it must be sorted out amid the realities and struggles of the here and now, whenever that happens to be. But what sociologist C. Wright Mills once said of Marx's ideas also seems relevant to those of Trotsky: 'To study his work today and then come back to our own concerns is to increase our chances of confronting them with useful ideas and solutions.'[16]

Long after his death, Trotsky's passion and ideas have continued to resonate. Whether they will again animate multitudes, reaching for a hopeful future, remains to be seen.

Dorothy Eisner, *Leon Trotsky II*, 1937, oil on canvas. Painted at the time of the Dewey Commission Hearings by an artist and sympathizer who was on the scene.

Chronology

1879 Born 7 November in the village of Yanovka (Ukraine)

1896 As student, moves to Nikolayev, encountering socialist ideas

1897 After briefly attending Odessa University, returns to Nikolayev, helping organize among workers

1898 Arrested and sent to prison, then Siberia, for revolutionary activity. Marries Alexandra Sokolovskya; they have two daughters

1902 Escapes from Siberia using the name Trotsky, permanently separating from Sokolovskya. Travels to London, joining Russian Social Democrats and working with Lenin

1903 At Second Congress of the Russian Social Democrats, held in London and Brussels, sides with the Menshevik faction against Lenin's Bolsheviks. Becomes involved with Natalia Sedova; they have two sons

1904 Breaks from Menshevik faction, maintaining independent stance among Russian Social Democrats

1905 Returns to Russia during revolutionary upsurge, becomes chair of St Petersburg Soviet of Workers' Deputies

1906 Arrested, tried, jailed. Writes *Results and Prospects*, expounding theory of permanent revolution

1907 Exiled to Siberia, but again escapes, settling in Vienna as a journalist

1912 Opposes effort to reorganize Russian Social Democrats under Bolshevik leadership, helps organize with Russian Social Democrats short-lived 'August bloc' of diverse factions and tendencies

1912–13 Serves as a war correspondent in Balkan Wars

1914 On eruption of First World War, joins other Russian Social Democrats, who condemn the war. Moves to France

1915 Writes 'Zimmerwald Manifesto' for international conference of anti-war socialists meeting in Switzerland

1916 Expelled from France for anti-war activity

1917 Arrives in New York in January, continuing anti-war efforts with other Russian émigrés. With outbreak of Russian Revolution (overthrow of Tsar), returns with his family to Russia, where he becomes a leader of a left-wing current among Russian Social Democrats that soon merges with Lenin's Bolsheviks. Elected chairman of Petrograd Soviet in September – and as most prominent Bolshevik next to Lenin, helps to organize successful Bolshevik Revolution (7 November). As Commissar of Foreign Affairs, begins negotiations with Germany at Brest-Litovsk to end Russia's involvement in the First World War

1918 After signing Brest-Litovsk Treaty, steps down as Commissar of Foreign Affairs, becoming Commissar of War. Building a new Red Army to fight in the Russian Civil War, he leads military struggle against innumerable efforts to overturn Russia's early Communist regime

1919 One of initial five members of Russian Communist Party's Political Bureau (Politburo). Plays a leading role in founding Communist International. Continues to lead Red Army in Civil War

1920 Civil War brought to a victorious end by Red Army. Writes *Terrorism and Communism*, defending extreme Communist measures of 'war communism'. With Lenin and others, advances 'united front' perspective at Second Congress of Communist International

1921 Clashes with Lenin over role of trade unions. Crisis in Russia leads to Kronstadt uprising of sailors and workers, which is suppressed

1922 With Lenin, forms 'bloc against bureaucracy' in Communist party and state, although Lenin is increasingly incapacitated by a series of strokes. Bloc of Zinoviev, Kamenev and Stalin forms in Politburo. Lenin warns in his *Testament* against the danger of a split in the Central Committee and calls for the removal of Stalin

1923 Trotsky's first open opposition to Stalin, *The New Course*, criticizes the bureaucratization of the Party and protests against violations of democracy and failure to develop adequate economic planning

1924 Lenin dies. 'Left Opposition' is condemned at the 13th Communist Party Conference. Writes *Lessons of October*, which includes a critical analysis of the role of Zinoviev and Kamenev in the Russian Revolution – provoking campaign on 'Errors of Trotskyism'

1925 Resigns as Commissar of War. Among works written and published from 1923 to 1925 are *Literature and Revolution*, *Problems of Everyday Life*, *Where is Britain Going?* and *On Lenin*

1926 Forms United Opposition with Zinoviev, Kamenev and others. They condemn growing bureaucracy, lack of democracy, inadequate economic development and Stalin's doctrine of 'socialism in one country'

1927 Massacre of Chinese Communists by Chiang Kai-shek vindicates Trotsky's critique of Stalinist policy there. Expelled with other Oppositionists from the Party. Trotsky's ailing friend Adolf Joffe commits suicide in protest, generating a mass rally at his funeral.

1928 Banished to Alma-Ata in Central Asia. Daughter Nina dies

1929 Exiled from the USSR to Turkey, settling on island of Prinkipo (Buyukada), near Istanbul. Begins to publish Russian-language *Bulletin of the Opposition*

1930 Publishes *My Life* and *Permanent Revolution*

1931–3 Publishes *History of the Russian Revolution*. Daughter Zina and grandson Seva visit from USSR. Trotsky and family stripped of Soviet citizenship. Gives major address 'In Defense of October' in Copenhagen, Denmark

1933 Daughter Zina commits suicide. Hitler takes power in Germany. Trotsky calls for Fourth International. Moves to France

1934 Assassination of Sergei Kirov in the USSR sets the stage for an intensification of repression

1935 Expelled from France, accepted into Norway. Critiques new 'People's Front' orientation of Communist International

1936 Publishes *The Revolution Betrayed*. Moscow trials begin, resulting in executions of many old Bolshevik leaders (including Zinoviev and Kamenev), with Trotsky and his activist son Lev condemned in absentia. Expelled from Norway. Spanish Civil War begins

1937 Trotsky arrives in Mexico, taking up residence near Mexico City. Son Sergei dies in Stalin's gulag amid mass executions of Left Oppositionists. Independent commission headed by John Dewey critically considers evidence of Moscow trials and issues verdict that Trotsky and others are 'not guilty'

1938 Son Lev dies under mysterious circumstances in Paris. Founding conference of Fourth International in France

1939 Hitler–Stalin Non-aggression Pact. Second World War begins. Trotsky works on biography *Stalin*

1940 Trotsky's house attacked by armed band led by Stalinist artist David Alfaro Siqueiros. Trotsky is unharmed. Three months later, on 21 August, he is assassinated by Stalinist agent Ramón Mercader

References

Introducing a Life

1 William Harlan Hale, 'When the Red Storm Broke', *American Heritage Magazine*, xii/2 (February 1961), p. 101. Also see Neil V. Salzman, *Reform and Revolution: The Life and Times of Raymond Robins* (Kent, OH, 1991).

2 Bertrand M. Patenaude, *Trotsky: Downfall of a Revolutionary* (New York, 2009), p. 8; Leon Trotsky, *The History of the Russian Revolution*, *Three Volumes in One* (New York, 1936), p. xvii.

3 John Reed, 'Ten Days that Shook the World', in *The Collected Works of John Reed* (New York, 1995), p. 633. Also see Robert A. Rosenstone, *Romantic Revolutionary: A Biography of John Reed* (New York, 1981).

4 Rick Geary, *Trotsky: A Graphic Biography* (New York, 2009), pp. 3–4.

5 Dmitri Volkogonov, *Trotsky: The Eternal Revolutionary* (New York, 1996), p. xxxii; Robert Service, *Trotsky: A Biography* (Cambridge, MA, 2009), p. 497.

6 Joshua Rubenstein, *Leon Trotsky: A Revolutionary's Life* (New Haven, CT, 2011), p. 209.

7 Max Eastman, *Heroes I Have Known: Twelve Who Lived Great Lives* (New York, 1942), p. 255; Slavoj Žižek, 'Foreword', in Leon Trotsky, *Terrorism and Communism* (London, 2007), p. viii; Peter Beilharz, *Trotsky, Trotskyism and the Transition to Socialism* (Totowa, NJ, 1987), p. 1; Geoffrey Swain, *Trotsky* (Harlow, 2006), p. 2.

8 Leon Trotsky, *Diary in Exile, 1935* (New York, 1963), pp. 46–7.

9 Beilharz, *Trotsky, Trotskyism and the Transition to Socialism*, pp. 10, 11; Žižek, 'Foreword', p. xxv.

10 Service, *Trotsky*, p. 403; Ian D. Thatcher, *Trotsky* (London, 2003), p. 187.

11 Thatcher, *Trotsky*, pp. 35–6, 102–3, 126, 184–5; 'A Letter from Geoffrey Swain and a Reply by David North', in David North, *Leon Trotsky and the Post-Soviet School of Historical Falsification* (Oak Park, MI, 2007), p. 84; Swain, *Trotsky*, pp. 57–121, 210, 211. I am definitely inclined, however, to agree that Trotsky sometimes tends to minimize the importance of roles played by others in historical events, particularly if they end up being political opponents.

12 Swain, *Trotsky*, pp. 2–3.

13 See E. H. Carr, *The Twilight of the Comintern, 1930–1935* (New York, 1982).

14 Swain, *Trotsky*, p. 157; Thatcher, *Trotsky*, pp. 9, 11.

15 Anatoly Lunacharsky, *Revolutionary Silhouettes* (New York, 1967), p. 60.

16 Leon Trotsky, *My Life: An Attempt at an Autobiography* (New York, 1970), p. 106.

17 'The Social Composition of the Party', *Writings of Leon Trotsky, 1936–37* (New York, 1978), pp. 489, 490.

18 William Reswick, *I Dreamt Revolution* (Chicago, 1952), p. 152; Trotsky, *My Life*, pp. 109, 110.

19 Quoted in V. Nevsky, 'Lev Davidovich Trotsky', in *Makers of the Russian Revolution: Biographies of Bolshevik Leaders*, ed. Georges Haupt and Jean-Jacques Marie (Ithaca, NY, 1974), p. 83; Max Eastman, *Leon Trotsky: The Portrait of a Youth* (New York, 1925), p. 46.

20 Leon Trotsky, *The Young Lenin* (New York, 1972), p. 187.

21 For discussions of Marxism consistent with what is presented here, see Phil Gasper, Karl Marx and Frederick Engels, *The Communist Manifesto: A Roadmap to History's Most Important Political Document* (Chicago, 2005); Paul Le Blanc, *From Marx to Gramsci* (Amherst, NY, 1996); August Nimtz, *Marx and Engels: Their Contribution to the Democratic Breakthrough* (Albany, NY, 2000); and Terry Eagleton, *Why Marx Was Right* (New Haven, CT, 2011). This summary is drawn from Paul Le Blanc and Michael D. Yates, *A Freedom Budget for All Americans: Recapturing the Promise of the Civil Rights Movement in the Struggle for Economic Justice Today* (New York, 2013), pp. 48–9.

22 Ziv quoted in Isaac Deutscher, *The Prophet Armed: Trotsky, 1879–1921* (New York, 1954), p. 35; Lunacharsky, *Revolutionary Silhouettes*, p. 67; Angelica Balabanoff, *My Life as a Rebel* (Bloomington, IN, 1973), p. 156.

23 Service, *Trotsky*, p. 52; Deutscher, *The Prophet Armed*, p. 35; Patenaude, *Trotsky*, p. 106; Lunacharsky, *Revolutionary Silhouettes*, p. 62.

24 Victor Serge and Natalia Sedova Trotsky, *The Life and Death of Leon Trotsky* (New York, 1975), pp. 121–3; Alice Rühle-Gerstel, 'No Verses for Trotsky: A Diary in Mexico (1937)', *Encounter* (April 1982), pp. 28, 31.

25 Serge and Sedova Trotsky, *The Life and Death of Leon Trotsky*, pp. 120–21; Sara Weber, 'Recollections of Trotsky', *Modern Occasions* (Spring 1972), pp. 185, 186.

26 Weber, 'Recollections of Trotsky', pp. 185–6.

27 N. N. Sukhanov, *The Russian Revolution, 1917: A Personal Account* (Princeton, NJ, 1984), pp. 584–5.

28 Erich Fromm, unpublished paper of 1958, from Erich Fromm Archives, reproduced in Marxist Internet Archive, www.marxists.org (accessed 23 December 2013).

29 Serge and Sedova Trotsky, *The Life and Death of Leon Trotsky*, pp. 123–4.

1 The Shock of Exile

1 Leon Trotsky, *My Life* (New York, 1970), p. 541; Victor Serge and Natalia Sedova Trotsky, *The Life and Death of Leon Trotsky* (New York, 1975), p. 156; Joel Carmichael, *Trotsky: An Appreciation of His Life* (New York, 1975), p. 351; Leon Trotsky, *Diary in Exile, 1935* (New York, 1963), p. 63.

2 After the name changed from Cheka to GPU, it became OGPU, then NKVD and finally KGB – but in this study we will, as did Trotsky, refer simply to the GPU.

3 On Dzerzhinsky, see Robert Blobaum, *Feliks Dzierzynski and the SDKPIL: A Study of the Origins of Polish Communism* (New York, 1984). On the Cheka, see George Leggett, *The Cheka: Lenin's Political Police* (New York, 1987). On what the revolutionary regime was dealing with, see William Henry Chamberlin, *The Russian Revolution*, vol. II: *1918–1921: From the Civil War to the Consolidation of Power* (Princeton, NJ, 1987); Michael Occleshaw, *Dances in Deep Shadows: The Clandestine War in Russia, 1917–20* (New York, 2006); David S.

Foglesong, *America's Secret War Against Bolshevism: u.s. Intervention in the Russian Civil War, 1917–1920* (Chapel Hill, NC, 1995).

4 Christopher Andrew and Oleg Gordievsky, *KGB: The Inside Story* (New York, 1990), p. 108.

5 Trotsky, *My Life*, p. 397; W. Bruce Lincoln, *Red Victory: A History of the Russian Civil War* (New York, 1989), pp. 295–6.

6 Lincoln, *Red Victory*, p. 189; Geoffrey Swain, *Russia's Civil War* (Stroud, Gloucestershire, 2008), p. 145; Trotsky, *My Life*, pp. 401, 407, 411.

7 Leon Trotsky, *Terrorism and Communism* (Ann Arbor, MI, 1961), pp. 62–3.

8 Trotsky, *Terrorism and Communism*, pp. 169–70. Arno J. Mayer's magisterial study *The Furies: Violence and Terror in the French and Russian Revolutions* (Princeton, NJ, 2000), p. 230, argues: 'Admittedly, the way the Bolsheviks took power was consistent with their credo of direct and defiant action, and their authoritarian rule following Red October was bound to provoke resistances which they were, of course, determined to counter and repress. But again, just as they were unprepared for the enormity of the crisis, so they were caught unawares by its Furies, which they were not alone to quicken.'

9 Rosa Luxemburg, 'The Russian Revolution', in *Socialism or Barbarism: The Selected Writings of Rosa Luxemburg*, ed. Paul Le Blanc and Helen C. Scott (London, 2010), p. 235; Leon Trotsky, 'Lessons of the Paris Commune' [4 February 1921], in *Leon Trotsky on the Paris Commune* (New York, 1970), p. 56.

10 Simon Pirani, *The Russian Revolution in Retreat, 1920–24: Soviet Workers and the New Communist Elite* (London, 2008), pp. 45, 53, 55, 91–2, 142.

11 'The Workers Opposition', in Alexandra Kollontai, *Selected Writings*, ed. Alix Holt (New York, 1980), pp. 169, 171.

12 See Diane P. Koenker, William G. Rosenberg and Ronald Grigor Suny, eds, *Party, State, and Society in the Russian Civil War: Explorations in Social History* (Bloomington, IN, 1989); Victor Serge, *Memoirs of a Revolutionary* (New York, 2012), pp. 144–55; and Paul Avrich, *Kronstadt 1921* (New York, 1974).

13 V. I. Lenin, 'The Party Crisis', in *Revolution, Democracy, Socialism: Selected Writings*, ed. Paul Le Blanc (London, 2008), p. 336.

14 See Lenin, *Revolution, Democracy, Socialism*, pp. 320–452; George Fyson, ed., *Lenin's Final Fight, 1922–23: Speeches and Writings* (New York, 1995); Moshe Lewin, *Lenin's Last Struggle* (Ann Arbor, MI, 2005).

15 Joseph Berger, *Shipwreck of a Generation* (London, 1971), pp. 70–71.

16 Hannah Arendt, *The Origins of Totalitarianism* (New York, 1958), p. 319.

17 Among the eyewitnesses, some more and some less critical-minded, were Roger N. Baldwin, *Liberty Under the Soviets* (New York, 1928); William H. Chamberlin, *Soviet Russia: A Living Record and a History* (Boston, 1930); Stuart Chase, Robert Dunn and Rexford Guy Tugwell, eds, *Soviet Russia in the Second Decade* (New York, 1928); John Dewey, *Impression of Soviet Russia and the Revolutionary World* (New York, 1929); Theodore Dreiser, *Dreiser Looks at Russia* (New York, 1928); Samuel Northrup Harper, *Civic Training in Soviet Russia* (Chicago, 1929); Julius F. Hecker, *Religion Under the Soviets* (New York, 1927); and Dorothy Thompson, *The New Russia* (New York, 1928). This is corroborated by later scholarship: Vladimir Brovkin, *Russia After Lenin: Politics, Culture and Society, 1921–1929* (London, 1998); William J. Chase, *Workers, Society, and the Soviet State: Labor and Life in Moscow, 1918–1929* (Urbana, IL, 1987); Sheila Fitzpatrick, Alexander Rabinowitch and Richard Stites, eds, *Russia in the Era of NEP: Explorations in Soviet Society and Culture* (Bloomington, IN, 1991); and Lewis W. Siegelbaum, *Soviet State and Society Between Revolutions, 1918–1929* (Cambridge, 1992).

18 Isaac Deutscher, *The Prophet Unarmed: Trotsky, 1921–1929* (Oxford, 1959), pp. 51, 53, 54, 78.

19 Leon Trotsky, *Our Political Tasks* (London, n.d.), pp. 72, 77.

20 Leon Trotsky, 'The New Course', in *The Challenge of the Left Opposition, 1923–25*, ed. Naomi Allen (New York, 1975), pp. 127, 134–5.

21 Information on post-Lenin developments, the Left Opposition and the campaign against 'Trotskyism' can be found in Max Eastman, *Since Lenin Died* (New York, 1925); Valentina Vilkova, ed., *The Struggle for Power: Russia in 1923* (Amherst, NY, 1996); Deutscher, *The Prophet Unarmed*, pp. 75–163; Serge and Sedova Trotsky, *The Life and Death of Leon Trotsky*, pp. 111–34; Trotsky, *My Life*, pp. 502–17; and Tony Cliff, *Trotsky*, vol. III: *Fighting the Rising Stalinist Bureaucracy, 1923–1927* (London, 1991), pp. 21–59.

22 *The Errors of Trotskyism: A Symposium* (London, 1925), available on the Marxist Internet Archive at http://marxists.anu.edu.au.

23 Trotsky, *The Challenge of the Left Opposition, 1923–25*, pp. 305, 310–15; Deutscher, *The Prophet Unarmed*, p. 139; Robert H. McNeal, *Bride of the Revolution: Krupskaya and Lenin* (London, 1973), pp. 247, 253, 258; Max Eastman, *Heroes I Have Known: Twelve Who Lived Great Lives* (New York, 1942), p. 243; Leon Trotsky, *Diary in Exile, 1935* (New York, 1963), p. 33.

24 'Declaration of the Thirteen', in Leon Trotsky, *The Challenge of the Left Opposition, 1926–1927*, ed. Naomi Allen and George Saunders (New York, 1980), pp. 77, 78, 80, 86.

25 E. H. Carr, *Socialism in One Country, 1924–1926*, vol. III, Part I (London, 1964), p. 19. On Britain, see Scott Nearing, *The British General Strike* (New York, 1926); G.D.H. Cole, *A History of the Labour Party from 1914* (New York, 1969), pp. 172–223; Christopher Farman, *The General Strike, May 1926* (London, 1972); and Leon Trotsky, *On Britain* (New York, 1973). On China, see Harold R. Isaacs, *The Tragedy of the Chinese Revolution* (Chicago, 2010); Benjamin I. Schwartz, *Chinese Communism and the Rise of Mao* (Cambridge, 1951); Alexander Pantsov, *The Bolsheviks and the Chinese Revolution, 1919–1927* (New York, 2000); and Leon Trotsky, *On China* (New York, 1976).

26 'Declaration of the Thirteen', pp. 74, 76, 81, 82, 84, 87, 89.

27 Serge and Sedova Trotsky, *The Life and Death of Leon Trotsky*, p. 144; Trotsky, *My Life*, pp. 531, 532; Deutscher, *The Prophet Unarmed*, pp. 274, 300.

28 Joseph Freeman, *An American Testament: A Narrative of Rebels and Romantics* (New York, 1936), pp. 628–30.

29 Trotsky, *Diary in Exile*, p. 24; McNeal, pp. 258, 259–60.

30 Michal Reiman, *The Birth of Stalinism* (Bloomington, IN, 1987), pp. 30–31.

31 Trotsky, *My Life*, pp. 533–4; Serge and Sedova Trotsky, *The Life and Death of Leon Trotsky*, p. 151; Deutscher, *The Prophet Unarmed*, pp. 372–7; Reiman, *The Birth of Stalinism*, pp. 33, 34.

32 Serge, *Memoirs*, p. 270; Boris Souvarine, *Stalin: A Critical Survey of Bolshevism* (New York, 1939), p. 476.

33 'In Memory of A. A. Joffe', in Trotsky, *The Challenge of the Left Opposition, 1926–1927*, p. 472; Trotsky, *My Life*, pp. 534–7.

34 Thompson, *The New Russia*, p. 306; Pierre Broué, 'Trotsky: A Biographer's Problems', in *The Trotsky Reappraisal*, ed. Terry Brotherstone and Paul Dukes (Edinburgh, 1992); Serge, *Memoirs of a Revolutionary*, p. 272; Serge and Sedova Trotsky, *The Life and Death of Leon Trotsky*, p. 155.

35 Serge and Sedova Trotsky, *The Life and Death of Leon Trotsky*, p. 156; Trotsky, *My Life*, pp. 539–40; Deutscher, *The Prophet Unarmed*, p. 393.

36 Leon Trotsky, *The Third International After Lenin* (New York, 1970), pp. 45–6; Bryan Palmer, *James P. Cannon and the Origins of the American Revolutionary Left, 1890–1928* (Urbana, IL, 2007), pp. 316–49.

37 Trotsky, *My Life*, p. 556; Serge and Sedova Trotsky, *The Life and Death of Leon Trotsky*, pp. 158–60. A rich account of the Oppositionists in 1928 can be found in chapter 35 of Pierre Broué's massive biography *Trotsky* (Paris, 1988), which appears in English translation as 'The Bolshevik-Leninist Faction', in *Revolutionary History*, IX/4 (2007), pp. 135–58.

38 Stephen Cohen, *Bukharin and the Bolshevik Revolution: A Political Biography, 1888–1938* (New York, 1975), p. 304; Reiman, *The Birth of Stalinism*, p. 99.

2 Revolutionary, Past and Present

1 Victor Serge and Natalia Sedova Trotsky, *The Life and Death of Leon Trotsky* (New York, 1975), p. 164; Sara Weber, 'Recollections of Trotsky', *Modern Occasion*, I/1 (Spring 1972), p. 182; Max Eastman, *Love and Revolution: My Journey through an Epoch* (New York, 1964), pp. 562–3.

2 Jean van Heijenoort, *With Trotsky in Exile: From Prinkipo to Coyoacán* (Cambridge, MA, 1978), pp. 13, 14; Weber, 'Recollections of Trotsky', pp. 182, 183; Serge and Sedova Trotsky, *The Life and Death of Leon Trotsky*, p. 165.

3 Eastman, *Love and Revolution*, p. 361; Max Eastman, *Heroes I Have Known: Twelve Who Lived Great Lives* (New York, 1942), p. 246. With slightly different wording, Sokolovskaya's comments are reproduced in Max Eastman, *Leon Trotsky: The Portrait of a Youth* (New York, 1925), p. 87.

4   Serge and Sedova Trotsky, *The Life and Death of Leon Trotsky*, p. 180.
    On the *Bulletin of the Left Opposition*, see the website of Wolfgang
    Lubitz, www.trotskyana.net (11 December 2013).

5   Serge and Sedova Trotsky, *The Life and Death of Leon Trotsky*, p. 180;
    Pierre Broué, 'The Bloc of the "Oppositions" against Stalin in the USSR
    in 1932', *Revolutionary History*, IX/4 (2007), p. 162.

6   M. Lewin, *Russian Peasants and Soviet Power: A Study of Collectivization*
    (New York, 1975), pp. 482–513; Donald Filtzer, *Soviet Workers and
    Stalinist Industrialization* (London, 1986), pp. 68–87; Aleksandra
    Chumkova, 'Memoirs', in *Samizdat: Voices of Soviet Opposition*, ed.
    George Saunders (New York, 1974), pp. 189–94; Kevin Murphy,
    *Revolution and Counterrevolution: Class Struggle in a Moscow Metal
    Factory* (Chicago, 2007), pp. 207–17; letter quoted in Boris Starkov,
    'Trotsky and Ryutin: From the History of the Anti-Stalinist Resistance
    in the 1930s', in *The Trotsky Appraisal*, ed. Terry Brotherstone and Paul
    Dukes (Edinburgh, 1992), p. 77; Charters Wynn, 'The "Right
    Opposition" and the "Smirnov-Eismont-Tolmachev Affair", in *The
    Lost Politburo Transcripts: From Collective Rule to Stalin's Dictatorship*,
    ed. Paul R. Gregory and Norman Naimark (New Haven, CT, 2008),
    p. 103.

7   Leon Trotsky, 'On the State of the Left Opposition', *Writings of Leon
    Trotsky, 1932–33*, ed. George Breitman and Sarah Lovell (New York,
    1972), pp. 33–4.

8   Wynn, 'The "Right Opposition" and the "Smirnov-Eismont-
    Tolmachev Affair", pp. 98, 99; Sobhanlal Datta Gupta, ed., *The Ryutin
    Platform: Stalin and the Crisis of Proletarian Dictatorship, Platform of the
    'Union of Marxists-Leninists'* (Kolkata, India, 2010), pp. 73, 74, 123, 138.

9   In addition to Broué, 'The Bloc of the "Oppositions" against Stalin',
    Starkov, 'Trotsky and Ryutin: From the History of the Anti-Stalinist
    Resistance in the 1930s', and Wynn, 'The "Right Opposition" and the
    "Smirnov-Eismont-Tolmachev Affair", see Serge and Sedova Trotsky,
    The Life and Death of Leon Trotsky, pp. 175–80, and Vadim Z. Rogovin,
    1937: Stalin's Year of Terror (Oak Park, MI, 1998), pp. 52–66.

10 Pierre Frank, *The Fourth International: The Long March of the Trotskyists*
    (London, 1979), p. 24.

11 Shachtman and Glotzer quoted in Robert J. Alexander, *International
    Trotskyism, 1929–1985: A Documented Analysis of the Movement*

(Durham, NC, 1991), pp. 25, 26; James P. Cannon, 'Leon Trotsky: To the Memory of the Old Man', in *Speeches for Socialism* (New York, 1971), pp. 181, 185. On Trotsky's interventions in U.S. and French contexts, see James P. Cannon, Max Shachtman, Leon Trotsky et al., *Dog Days: James P. Cannon vs. Max Shachtman in the Communist League of America, 1931–1933* (New York, 2002), and Leon Trotsky, *Crisis in the French Section, 1935–36*, ed. Naomi Allen and George Breitman (New York, 1977). On organizational theory, see Dianne Feeley, Paul Le Blanc and Thomas Twiss, *Leon Trotsky and the Organizational Principles of the Revolutionary Party* (Chicago, 2014).

12 Serge and Sedova Trotsky, *The Life and Death of Leon Trotsky*, p. 165.

13 Isaac Deutscher, *The Prophet Outcast, Trotsky: 1929–1940* (London, 1963), pp. 221, 222, 229; Ronald Segal, *Leon Trotsky* (New York, 1979), p. 325.

14 Leon Trotsky, *The History of the Russian Revolution: Three Volumes in One* (New York, 1936), pp. 5–6. Summary drawn from Paul Le Blanc, 'Uneven and Combined Development and the Sweep of History', *International Viewpoint* (2005), www.internationalviewpoint.org.

15 Michael Löwy, *The Politics of Combined and Uneven Development: The Theory of Permanent Revolution* (Chicago, 2010), pp. 43, 101; Richard B. Day and Daniel F. Gaido, eds, *Witnesses to Permanent Revolution, The Documentary Record* (Chicago, 2011), p. xi. Lenin's reference to 'uninterrupted revolution' can be found in 'Social-Democracy's Attitude Toward the Peasant Movement', *Collected Works*, vol. IX (Moscow, 1962), pp. 236–7; also see Nadezhda Krupskaya's discussion of the evolution of his thinking in 1915–16 regarding the linkage of democratic and socialist revolutions in N. K. Krupskaya, *Reminiscences of Lenin* (New York, 1970), pp. 328–30. Teodor Shanin, *Late Marx and the Russian Road: Marx and the Peripheries of Capitalism* (New York, 1983) documents Marx himself inclining toward a 'permanentist' approach in analysing revolutionary possibilities in late nineteenth-century Russia. In their 'Address of the Central Committee to the Communist League' of March 1850 (which concludes that the workers' 'battle cry must be: The Permanent Revolution'), Marx and Engels lay out the basic perspective, but key elements can also be traced in their *Communist Manifesto* – see Karl Marx, *Political Writings*, vol. I: *The Revolutions of 1848*, ed. David Fernbach (London, 1973), pp. 86–7, 98,

319–30. In *Karl Marx and Friedrich Engels: An Introduction to Their Lives and Work* (New York, 1973), Bolshevik archivist and historian David Riazanov notes that the circulars of 1850 happened to be 'precisely' what 'Lenin, who knew them by heart, used to delight in quoting' (p. 100).

16 Löwy, *The Politics of Combined and Uneven Development*, p. 40; Isaac Deutscher, 'Trotsky in Our Time', in *Marxism in Our Time*, ed. Tamara Deutscher (San Francisco, CA, 1973), p. 36.

17 Summary drawn from Le Blanc, 'Uneven and Combined Development and the Sweep of History'.

18 Leon Trotsky, *The Permanent Revolution & Results and Prospects* (London, 2007), pp. 253–4.

19 Some interpreters of Trotsky's theory are inclined to insist on a more restrictive understanding of the permanent revolution perspective – as applying exclusively to the possibility and necessity of *economically less developed countries* linking democratic with socialist revolutions in order to forge a path to modernity and freedom, albeit in the context of a global revolutionary process. While seeing this as one key dimension of Trotsky's orientation, I believe that Deutscher's expansive understanding is more apt – that *permanent revolution* involves, rather, 'the quintessential element' of Marxism, therefore having more general application.

Obviously distorting Trotsky's meaning is Stalin's contention ('The October Revolution and the Tactics of the Russian Communists' in *Problems of Leninism* [Beijing, 1976], p. 132, italics added) that it is 'the theory of *simultaneous victory of socialism* in the principal countries of Europe which, as a rule, excludes Lenin's theory of revolution about the victory of socialism in one country.' This description of Trotsky's theory simply doesn't hold up when we consider what Trotsky actually said – which, however, certainly *does* exclude Stalin's notion of 'socialism in one country' (economically backward Russia), which Stalin falsely attributes to Lenin.

More sophisticated is Peter Beilharz, *Trotsky, Trotskyism and the Transition to Socialism* (Towota, NJ, 1987), p. 27: 'The theory itself has two parts. The first . . . is that bourgeois revolutions become, in the twentieth century, impossible: they may be initiated as bourgeois revolutions, but *can only result* in proletarian revolutions. The second

. . . is that, because international capital breaks through the relations of the nation-state, revolution also becomes *necessarily* international' [italics added]. Beilharz says that 'as capitalist civilization slides into the twenty-first century, it can only be observed that Trotsky's conclusions . . . were hopelessly wide of the mark.' Yet the italicized words indicate notions of inevitability absent from Trotsky's analysis, which Beilharz converts from a discussion of revolutionary dynamics into a sterile prophecy.

20 Leon Trotsky, 'What Next? Vital Questions for the German Proletariat', in *The Struggle Against German Fascism*, ed. George Breitman and Merry Maisel (New York, 1971), p. 213.

21 Valuable contextualization is provided in Evelyn Anderson, *Hammer or Anvil: The Story of the German Working-class Movement* (London, 1945); Franz Neumann, *Behemoth: The Structure and Practice of National Socialism, 1933–1944* (Chicago, 2009); Geoff Eley, *Forging Democracy: The History of the Left in Europe, 1850–2000* (New York, 2002); and Geoff Eley, *Nazism as Fascism: Violence, Ideology, and the Ground of Consent in Germany, 1930–1945* (New York, 2013).

22 Trotsky, 'What Next', p. 254.

23 On the loss of the Marx–Engels work, see Leon Trotsky, *Trotsky's Diary in Exile, 1935* (New York, 1963), p. 11. On Seva with matches, see Deutscher, *The Prophet Outcast*, p. 149. On speculations regarding Zina, see Robert Service, *Trotsky, A Biography* (Cambridge, MA, 2009), claiming that 'strong suspicion fell upon Zina' for the fires (p. 385); Service cites Albert Glotzer, *Trotsky: Memoir and Critique* (Buffalo, NY, 1989), who in a reference note (p. 85 n34) refers to Joel Carmichael, *Trotsky: An Appreciation of His Life* (New York, 1975) for his own assertion that 'members of the household believed her to be responsible for the fires'. This is not corroborated by the source: Carmichael writes that 'within the first few months after Zinaida's arrival fire swept the household twice', but without mentioning or suggesting suspicions about Zina starting the fires (p. 401). Glotzer seems to have misread his source, and Service simply repeats his mistake. Clarifications on what actually happened are provided in a communication to the author from Esteban Volkow, 9 July 2014, repeated in a face-to-face interview on 19 July 2014, which corroborates Van Heijenoort, *With Trotsky in Exile*, pp. 24–5.

24 Van Heijenoort, *With Trotsky in Exile*, p. 34.
25 Telephone calls are emphasized in Segal, *Leon Trotsky*, p. 344.
   Additional information regarding Zina is provided in Dmitri
   Volkogonov, *Trotsky: The Eternal Revolutionary* (New York, 1996),
   pp. 348–52, and especially in Van Heijenoort, *With Trotsky in Exile*,
   pp. 35–7.

3 The Revolution Betrayed

1 Gustav Regler, *The Owl of Minerva* (New York, 1959), p. 135.
2 'Farewell to Prinkipo', in *Writings of Leon Trotsky, 1932–33*, ed. George
   Breitman and Sarah Lovell (New York, 1972), pp. 312, 318.
3 Alfred Rosmer, 'On the Planet Without a Visa', in Alfred Rosmer, Boris
   Souvarine, Emile Fabrol and Antoine Clavez, *Trotsky and the Origins of
   Trotskyism* (London, 2002), p. 155; Victor Serge and Natalia Sedova
   Trotsky, *The Life and Death of Leon Trotsky* (New York, 1975), pp. 193–4.
4 Oddvar K. Høidal, *Trotsky in Norway: Exile, 1935–1937* (DeKalb, IL,
   2013), pp. 37–40; Serge and Sedova Trotsky, *The Life and Death of Leon
   Trotsky*, pp. 208, 209.
5 Richard Greeman, 'The Victor Serge Affair and the French Literary
   Left', *Revolutionary History*, V/3 (1994), pp. 142–74; David James
   Fisher, *Romain Rolland and the Politics of Intellectual Engagement*
   (Berkeley, CA, 1988), p. 274.
6 Sara Weber, 'Recollections of Trotsky', *Modern Occasions*, I/1 (Spring
   1972), p. 187; Jean van Heijenoort, *With Trotsky in Exile: From Prinkipo
   to Coyoacán* (Cambridge, MA, 1978), p. 54.
7 Simone Pétrement, *Simone Weil: A Life* (New York, 1976), pp. 176, 178,
   188–9; Trotsky, 'The Class Nature of the Soviet State', *Writings of Leon
   Trotsky, 1933–34*, ed. George Breitman and Bev Scott (New York, 1975),
   p. 114.
8 Pétrement, *Simone Weil*, p. 178.
9 A meticulous account is provided in George Breitman, 'The Rocky
   Road to the Fourth International, 1933–38', in *Malcolm X and the Third
   American Revolution: The Writings of George Breitman*, ed. Anthony
   Marcus (Amherst, NY, 2005), pp. 299–352. Also see Pierre Frank, *The
   Fourth International: The Long March of the Trotskyists* (London, 1979),

pp. 43–57; Robert J. Alexander, *International Trotskyism, 1929–1985: A Documented Analysis of the Movement* (Durham, NC, 1991), pp. 251–84.

10 Georgi Dimitroff, *The United Front: The Struggle Against Fascism and War* (New York, 1938), p. 110.

11 Ernst Fischer, *An Opposing Man* (New York, 1974), p. 267; Louis Fischer, *Men and Politics, An Autobiography* (New York, 1941), pp. 308, 311; E. H. Carr, *The Twilight of the Comintern, 1930–1935* (New York, 1982), pp. 419, 426; Paulo Spriano, *Stalin and the European Communists* (London, 1985), p. 16.

12 Spriano, *Stalin and the European Communists*, p. 19. See also David Caute, *The Fellow-travellers: A Postscript to the Enlightenment* (New York, 1973), especially pp. 132–84.

13 Trotsky, 'The Trial of the Twenty-one', *Writings of Leon Trotsky, 1937–38*, ed. Naomi Allen and George Breitman (New York, 1976), pp. 186–7; Theodore Dan, *The Origins of Bolshevism* (New York, 1970), p. 406.

14 See *The Case of Leon Trotsky* (New York, 1969), pp. 298, 386; *Leon Trotsky on France*, ed. David Salner (New York, 1979); Leon Trotsky, *The Spanish Revolution, 1931–39*, ed. Naomi Allen and George Breitman (New York, 1973).

15 Leon Trotsky, *The Revolution Betrayed* (New York, 1972), p. 56; Karl Marx, 'The German Ideology', in *Writings of the Young Marx on Philosophy and Society*, ed. Loyd Easton and Kurt H. Guddat (Garden City, NY, 1967), p. 427; Karl Marx and Frederick Engels, 'Preface to the Second Russian Edition of the *Manifesto of the Communist Party*', in *Late Marx and the Russian Road: Marx and the 'Peripheries of Capitalism'*, ed. Teodor Shanin (New York, 1983), p. 139.

16 Trotsky, *The Revolution Betrayed*, pp. 59, 112.

17 Ibid., pp. 113, 120.

18 Ibid., p. 255.

19 Ibid., p. 288.

20 Ibid., pp. 289–90.

21 Commission of the Central Committee of the CPSU (B), ed., *History of the Communist Party of the Soviet Union (Bolsheviks): Short Course* (New York, 1939), pp. 330, 346–7. On issues related to the 50 accused/ thirteen on trial question, see Serge and Sedova Trotsky, *The Life and Death of Leon Trotsky*, pp. 202–3. Information on the Kirov assassination, its investigation and its consequences can be

found in Oleg V. Khlevniuk, *Master of the House: Stalin and his Inner Circle* (New Haven, CT, 2009), pp. 66–8, 127–202, J. Arch Getty and Oleg V. Naumov, *Yezhov: The Rise of Stalin's 'Iron Fist'* (New Haven, CT, 2008), pp. 135–78, and Matthew E. Lenoe, *The Kirov Murder and Soviet History* (New Haven, CT, 2010). A brilliant initial response by Trotsky's son, composed while Trotsky was still muzzled under what amounted to house arrest in Norway, can be found in Leon Sedov, *The Red Book on the Moscow Trial* (London, 1980), accessible via the Marxist Internet Archive at www.marxists.org, accessed 24 October 2014. Also see Robert Conquest, *The Great Terror: A Reassessment* (New York, 2008), and Roy Medvedev, *Let History Judge: The Origins and Consequences of Stalinism* (New York, 1989).

22 Fischer, *An Opposing Man*, pp. 504–5.

23 Vadim Z. Rogovin, *1937: Stalin's Year of Terror* (Oak Park, MI, 1998), pp. 60–66.

24 Fischer, *An Opposing Man*, pp. 305, 306.

25 Victor Serge, 'Confession', in *Resistance: Poems by Victor Serge* (San Francisco, CA, 1989), pp. 22–3.

26 Serge and Sedova Trotsky, *The Life and Death of Leon Trotsky*, p. 205; Maria Joffe, *One Long Night: A Tale of Truth* (London, 1978), p. 178; Moshe Lewin, *The Soviet Century* (London, 2005), pp. 106–7; Vadim M. Rogovin, *Stalin's Terror of 1937–1938* (Oak Park, MI, 2009), pp. 446–7. Also see Oleg V. Khlevniuk, *The History of the Gulag: From Collectivization to the Great Terror* (New Haven, CT, 2004).

27 Serge and Sedova Trotsky, *The Life and Death of Leon Trotsky*, p. 202.

28 Robert C. Tucker, *Stalin in Power: The Revolution from Above, 1928–1941* (New York, 1992), pp. 8–9, 65.

29 Joffe, *One Long Night*, pp. 162, 190.

30 Nadezhda A. Joffe, *Back in Time: My Life, My Fate, My Epoch* (Oak Park, MI, 1995), pp. 66, 70.

31 Victor Serge, *From Lenin to Stalin* (New York, 1973), p. 66; Joffe, *Back in Time*, p. 71; Isabelle Longuet, *La Crise de L'Opposition de gauche en 1928–1929* (Paris, 1987), Isabelle Longuet, *Mémoire de Maitrise*, Université de Paris VIII, cited in Tony Cliff, *Trotsky: The Darker the Night the Brighter the Star, 1927–1940*, vol. IV (London, 1993), p. 97.

32 John Marot, *The October Revolution in Prospect and Retrospect, Interventions in Russian and Soviet History* (Chicago, 2013), p. 89;

Thomas M. Twiss, 'Trotsky's Analysis of Stalinism', *Critique*, 54 (December 2010), p. 551. Also see the brilliant exploration of Trotsky's evolving analysis in Thomas M. Twiss, *Trotsky and the Problem of Soviet Bureaucracy* (Boston and Leiden, 2014).

33 Joffe, *Back in Time*, p. 84.

34 'Memoirs of a Bolshevik-Leninist', in *Samizdat: Voices of the Soviet Opposition*, ed. George Saunders (New York, 1974), p. 141.

35 Joseph Berger, *Shipwreck of a Generation* (London, 1971), pp. 94–5.

36 M. B., 'Trotskyists at Vorkuta, An Eyewitness Report', in *Samizdat*, p. 206.

37 Ibid., pp. 210–11.

38 Joffe, *One Long Night*, pp. 40–41.

39 M. B. in Saunders, *Samizdat*, pp. 215, 216; Berger, *Shipwreck of a Generation*, pp. 96–8.

40 Joffe, *One Long Night*, pp. 186–7; Rogovin, *Stalin's Terror of 1937–1938*, pp. 281–6.

41 Mikhail Baitalsky, *Notebooks for the Grandchildren: Recollections of a Trotskyist Who Survived the Stalin Terror* (Atlantic Highlands, NJ, 1995), p. 225.

42 Berger, *Shipwreck of a Generation*, pp. 94, 95; Serge and Sedova Trotsky, *The Life and Death of Leon Trotsky*, pp. 218–19. On the survival of Sergei's wife and daughter (and the latter's utter rejection of what passed for Communism and Marxism), see Yulia Akselrod, 'Why My Grandfather Leon Trotsky Must Be Turning in His Grave', *Commentary* (April 1989), pp. 39–43.

43 Joffe, *Back in Time*, p. 102; Rogovin, *1937: Stalin's Year of Terror*, pp. 387, 388.

44 Joffe, *One Long Night*, 190.

45 Deutscher, *The Prophet Outcast*, p. 292; Serge and Sedova Trotsky, *The Life and Death of Leon Trotsky*, pp. 208–9; Høidal, *Trotsky in Norway*, pp. 238, 254, 262.

4 Bracing for the Storm

1 Bernard Wolfe, *Memoirs of a Not Altogether Shy Pornographer* (Garden City, NJ, 1972), pp. 33–4.

2 Dmitri Volkogonov, *Trotsky: The Eternal Revolutionary* (New York, 1996), p. 363; Pavel Sudoplatov, Anatoli Pavel Sudoplatov, with Jerrold L. and Leona P. Schecter, *Special Tasks: The Memoirs of an Unwanted Witness – A Soviet Spymaster* (Boston, MA, 1994), p. 67; Mary-Kay Wilmers, *The Eitingons: A Twentieth-century Story* (London, 2010), who sums up Stalin's comments on p. 289. The anonymous GPU agent was Alexander Orlov.

3 Serge and Sedova Trotsky, *The Life and Death of Leon Trotsky*, pp. 226–7; Jean van Heijenoort, *With Trotsky in Exile: From Prinkipo to Coyoacán* (Cambridge, MA, 1978), p. 134; Joseph Hansen, 'With Trotsky in Coyoacan', in Leon Trotsky, *My Life* (New York, 1970), p. xviii.

4 On the ILD, see Bryan D. Palmer, *James P. Cannon and the Origins of the American Revolutionary Left, 1890–1928* (Urbana, IL, 2007), pp. 252–84; for the Sacco and Vanzetti case, Bruce Watson, *Sacco and Vanzetti: The Men, the Murders, and the Judgment of Mankind* (New York, 2007), and Susan Tejada, *In Search of Sacco and Vanzetti: Double Lives, Troubled Times, and the Massachusetts Murder Case that Shook the World* (Boston, MA, 2012).

5 Max Shachtman, 'The Trotsky I Knew (Extracts from Max Shachtman's Autobiography)', *Workers' Liberty*, www.workersliberty.org (accessed 24 December 2013); James P. Cannon, 'To the Memory of the Old Man', in *James P. Cannon, Writings and Speeches, 1940–43: The Socialist Workers Party in World War II*, ed. Les Evans (New York, 1975), p. 56.

6 Rae Spiegel/Raya Dunayevskaya, 'The Man Trotsky', unpublished manuscript (approximately 1938), p. 20 (thanks to Peter Hudis for sharing this); Hansen, 'With Trotsky in Coyoacan', pp. xii, xiii, xvii.

7 David North, *A Tribute to Harold Robins, Captain of Trotsky's Guard* (Detroit, MI, 1987), pp. 7–8.

8 Hansen, 'With Trotsky in Coyoacan', p. xiii.

9 George Breitman, ed., *Leon Trotsky on Black Nationalism and Self-determination* 2nd edn (New York, 1978), especially pp. 45–8; C.L.R. James, 'The Revolutionary Answer to the Negro Problem in the United States', in Scott McLemee, ed., *C.L.R. James on the 'Negro Question'* (Jackson, MS, 1996), pp. 138–47; Claude McKay, *A Long Way from Home: An Autobiography* (New York, 1970), p. 208.

10 Al Richardson, Ted Crawford et al., eds, *From Syndicalism to Trotskyism: Writings of Alfred and Marguerite Rosmer*, taking up

most of *Revolutionary History*, VII/4 (2000); Alice Rühle-Gerstel, 'No Verses for Trotsky, A Diary in Mexico (1937)', *Encounter* (April 1982), pp. 27–41; Otto Rühle Archive at Marxist Internet Archive, www.marxists.org/archive/ruhle; André Breton, *What is Surrealism?: Selected Writings*, ed. Franklin Rosemont (New York, 1978); 'Manifesto for an Independent Revolutionary Art', Marxist Internet Archive, www.marxists.org.

11 See Pierre Broué and Emil Temime, *The Revolution and Civil War in Spain, 1934–1939* (Chicago, 2008), and scholarly surveys by Helen Graham, *The Spanish Civil War, A Very Short Introduction* (New York, 2005) and Andy Durgan, *The Spanish Civil War* (London, 2007).

12 William Herrick, *Jumping the Line* (Oakland, CA, 2001), pp. 151–2.

13 'The Lessons of Spain: The Last Warning', in Leon Trotsky, *The Spanish Revolution, 1931–39*, ed. Naomi Allen and George Breitman (New York, 1973), pp. 308–9, 316; *The Case of Leon Trotsky* (New York, 1969), p. 296.

14 Isaac Deutscher, *The Prophet Outcast, Trotsky: 1929–1940* (London, 1963), pp. 386–97; Hugo Dewar, *Assassins at Large* (Boston, MA, 1952); Christopher Andrew and Oleg Gordievsky, *KGB: The Inside Story* (New York, 1990), pp. 157–72; Leon Trotsky, 'To the Editor of *Modern Monthly*', in *Writings of Leon Trotsky, 1936–37*, ed. Naomi Allen and George Breitman (New York, 1978), p. 498.

15 Deutscher, *The Prophet Outcast*, p. 482; *Writings of Leon Trotsky, 1939–40*, ed. Naomi Allen and George Breitman (New York, 1973), pp. 110–12, 130–38; William Chase, 'Trotsky in Mexico: Toward a History of His Discreet Contacts with the U.S. Government (1937–1940)', *Otechestvennaya istoriya* (*Native History*), 4 (1995), in Russian, partially reproduced online: www.situation.ru; Christopher Hitchens, '1984 and All That', *The Nation*, 24 August 1998.

16 See James T. Farrell, 'Dewey in Mexico', in Sidney Hook, ed., *John Dewey: Philosopher of Science and Freedom* (New York, 1950).

17 An outstanding account of the involvement of, and impact on, U.S. left-wing intellectuals can be found in Alan Wald, *The New York Intellectuals: The Rise and Decline of the Anti-Stalinist Left from the 1930s to the 1980s* (Chapel Hill, NC, 1987), especially pp. 128–63. The tilt of many left-wing and liberal intellectuals in the U.S. and Britain toward an acceptance of the Moscow trials is chronicled

in Frank A. Warren, *Liberals and Communism: The 'Red Decade'*
Revisited (Bloomington, IN, 1966), pp. 163–92, and Paul Flewers,
The New Civilization? Understanding Stalin's Soviet Union (London,
2008), pp. 145–54.

18 *Not Guilty: Report of the Commission of Inquiry into the Charges Made*
Against Leon Trotsky in the Moscow Trials (New York, 1972), p. xxi.
For decades stretching from the late 1930s, many millions embraced
the Stalinist account of the Moscow trials as proving Trotsky's
counter-revolutionary plotting – portrayed, for example, in an
internationally best-selling popularization by Michael Sayers and
Albert E. Kahn, *The Great Conspiracy against Russia* (New York,
1946), which was endorsed by many left-leaning liberals, including
certain prominent New Deal politicians. Pro-Stalin researchers
would replicate such accounts well into the twenty-first century –
see, for example, Grover Furr, *The Murder of Sergei Kirov: History,*
Scholarship and the Anti-Stalin Paradigm (Kettering, OH, 2013),
which argues that the defendants at the Moscow trials were guilty
as charged, along with Trotsky and a number of his supporters. Yet
Furr's methodology suffers from 'tendentious and one-sided reading
of the evidence . . . innuendos and speculation . . . overblown and
hyperbolic language, and . . . unsupported allegations', as one
semi-sympathetic critic puts it (Roger Keeran, 'Khrushchev Lied,
But What Is the Truth?', *Marxism-Leninism Today* (23 November
2011), http://mltoday.com.

19 George Novack, 'Introduction', in *The Case of Leon Trotsky*
(New York, 1969), pp. xii, xiii.

20 *The Case of Leon Trotsky*, pp. 436–7.

21 Ibid., pp. 584–5.

22 Deutscher, *The Prophet Outcast*, pp. 382–6; Van Heijenoort, *With*
Trotsky in Exile, pp. 112–14; Bertrand M. Patenaude, *Trotsky: Downfall*
of a Revolutionary (New York, 2009), pp. 59–72.

23 Van Heijenoort, *With Trotsky in Exile*, p. 114; Tracy B. Strong and Helene
Keyssar, *Right in Her Soul: The Life of Anna Louise Strong* (New York,
1983), pp. 91–3; Nadezhda Adolfovna Joffe, letter to editor, *Novoie*
russkoie slovo (18 March 1997), reproduced in English translation as
'Trotsky's Romances, Real and Imagined' by Iskra Research (5 May
1997), http://web.mit.edu; Robert Service, *Trotsky: A Biography*

(Cambridge, MA, 2009), pp. 265–6, regarding Sheridan, seems corroborated in Clare Sheridan, *From Mayfair to Moscow: Clare Sheridan's Diary* (New York, 1921), and Anita Leslie, *Clare Sheridan* (New York, 1977), pp. 142–6.

24 Meghan Delahunt, *In the Casa Azul: A Novel of Revolution and Betrayal* (New York, 2001), pp. 282, 283; Lillian Pollak, *The Sweetest Dream: Love, Lies, Assassination and Hope, A Novel of the Thirties*, repr. (Bloomington, IN, 2009), p. 142. For excerpts from Trotsky's passionate letters pressing toward reconciliation, see Alain Dugrand, *Trotsky in Mexico, 1937–1940* (Manchester, 1992), p. 20.

25 Leon Trotsky, *Diary in Exile, 1935* (New York, 1963), pp. 42–3.

26 Serge and Sedova Trotsky, *The Life and Death of Leon Trotsky*, p. 206.

27 Van Heijenoort, *With Trotsky in Exile*, p. 27; Pierre Broué, 'In Germany for the International (Excerpt from *Leon Sedov*)', *Revolutionary History*, IX/4 (2008), www.marxists.org; Dale Reed and Michael Jakobson, 'Trotsky Papers at the Hoover Institution: One Chapter of an Archival Mystery Story', *American Historical Review*, XCII/2 (1987), p. 366.

28 These are examined in considerable detail, from Trotsky's own standpoint (with an abundance of Trotsky quotes), in Dianne Feeley, Paul Le Blanc and Thomas Twiss, *Leon Trotsky and the Organizational Principles of the Revolutionary Party* (Chicago, 2014).

29 See especially Elisabeth K. Poretsky, *Our Own People: A Memoir of 'Ignace Reiss' and His Friends* (Ann Arbor, MI, 1970); also Serge and Sedova Trotsky, *The Life and Death of Leon Trotsky*, p. 255.

30 Rae Spiegel/Raya Dunayevskaya, 'The Man Trotsky', pp. 12–13; Hansen, 'With Trotsky in Coyoacan', p. xxiii.

31 'Open Letter for the Fourth International', in *Writings of Leon Trotsky, 1935–36*, ed. Naomi Allen and George Breitman (New York, 1977), pp. 27–8.

32 Isaac Deutscher, 'Internationals and Internationalism', in *Marxism in Our Time*, ed. Tamara Deutscher (Berkeley, CA, 1971), p. 108; 'The Way Out', in *The Writings of Leon Trotsky, 1934–35*, ed. George Breitman and Bev Scott (New York, 1974), p. 85; Van Heijenoort, *With Trotsky in Exile*, p. 130. On each, see Al Richardson, Ted Crawford et al., eds, *A Paradise for Capitalism? Class and Leadership in Twentieth-century Belgium*, special issue, *Revolutionary History*, VII/1 (1978), and Bryan

Palmer, *Revolutionary Teamsters: The Minneapolis Truckers' Strikes of 1934* (Leiden and Boston, 2013).

33 C.L.R. James, 'Trotsky's Place in History', in *C.L.R. James and Revolutionary Marxism: Selected Writings of C.L.R. James, 1939–1949*, ed. Scott McLemee and Paul Le Blanc (Atlantic Highlands, NJ, 1994), pp. 128–9.

34 'Review of the Conference' in *Documents of the Fourth International: The Formative Years, 1933–40*, ed. Will Reissner (New York, 1973), p. 157; Robert J. Alexander, *International Trotskyism, 1929–1985: A Documented Analysis of the Movement* (Durham, NC, 1991), p. 270.

35 Leon Trotsky, *The Transitional Program for Socialist Revolution* (New York, 1974), p. 111.

36 Peter Beilharz, *Trotsky, Trotskyism and the Transition to Socialism* (Totowa, NJ, 1987), pp. 75–6.

37 Ibid., p. 75.

38 Rosa Luxemburg, 'Reform or Revolution', in *Socialism or Barbarism: The Selected Writings of Rosa Luxemburg*, ed. Paul Le Blanc and Helen C. Scott (London, 2010), p. 48; V. I. Lenin, 'The Revolutionary Proletariat and the Rights of Nations to Self-determination', in *Revolution, Democracy, Socialism: Selected Writings*, ed. Paul Le Blanc (London, 2008), pp. 233–4. Also see Paul Le Blanc, *Marx, Lenin, and the Revolutionary Experience: Studies in Communism and Radicalism in the Age of Globalization* (New York, 2006), pp. 43–8.

39 Trotsky, *The Transitional Program*, p. 75.

40 Daniel Bensaïd, *Strategies of Resistance and 'Who Are the Trotskyists?'* (London, 2009), p. 23.

41 Trotsky, *The Transitional Program*, p. 112.

5 The Jaws of Death

1 Material here is drawn from Jerrold L. and Leona P. Schecter, *Special Tasks: The Memoirs of an Unwanted Witness – A Soviet Spymaster* (Boston, MA, 1994), pp. 69–74; Christopher Andrew and Vasili Mitrokhin, *The Sword and the Shield: The Mitrokhin Archive and the Secret History of the KGB* (New York, 1999), pp. 86–7; Mary-Kay Wilmers, *The Eitingons: A Twentieth-century Story* (London, 2010), pp. 296–8.

2 Rae Spiegel/Raya Dunayevskaya, 'The Man Trotsky', unpublished manuscript (approximately 1938), pp. 1–2.

3 Bertram D. Wolfe, *Memoirs of a Not Altogether Shy Pornographer* (Garden City, NJ, 1972), pp. 34–5.

4 Joseph Hansen, 'With Trotsky in Coyoacan', in Leon Trotsky, *My Life* (New York, 1970), p. xviii.

5 Ibid., pp. xiv–xv.

6 Ibid., p. xiii.

7 Rae Spiegel/Raya Dunayevskaya, 'The Man Trotsky', pp. 15–16.

8 'Imperialist War and the Proletarian Revolution', in *Documents of the Fourth International: The Formative Years, 1933–40*, ed. Will Reissner (New York, 1973), pp. 311, 325. Also see Wolfgang Leonhard, *Betrayal: The Hitler-Stalin Pact of 1939* (New York, 1989).

9 James T. Farrell, 'A Portrait of Leon Trotsky', *Partisan Review* (October 1940), reprinted in Alain Dugrand, *Trotsky in Mexico, 1937–1940* (Manchester, 1992), pp. 58–9.

10 'On the Threshold of a New World War', in *Writings of Leon Trotsky, 1936–37*, ed. Naomi Allen and George Breitman (New York, 1978), pp. 390, 391, 392, 393, 396.

11 Ibid., pp. 393, 394.

12 Ernest Mandel, *The Meaning of the Second World War* (London, 1986), p. 169.

13 Ibid., p. 45. Also see Ernest Mandel, 'Trotskyists and the Resistance in World War Two', in Pierre Frank, *The Fourth International: The Long March of the Trotskyists* (London, 1979), pp. 173–81.

14 Robert J. Alexander, *International Trotskyism, 1929–1985: A Documented Analysis of the Movement* (Durham, NC, 1991), pp. 285–304, 793–812; Leon Trotsky, *In Defense of Marxism* (New York, 1970).

15 See Alan Wald, *The New York Intellectuals: The Rise and Decline of the Anti-Stalinist Left from the 1930s to the 1980s* (Chapel Hill, NC, 1987).

16 Hansen, 'With Trotsky in Coyoacan', pp. xii–xiii.

17 Boris Souvarine, *Stalin: A Critical Survey of Bolshevism* (New York, 1939); Leon Trotsky, *Stalin: An Appraisal of the Man and His Influence* (New York, 1967), p. 54.

18 Trotsky, *Stalin*, pp. 53–4.

19 Ibid., p. 112.

20 James Burnham and Max Shachtman, 'Intellectuals in Retreat',
   New International (January 1939), pp. 3–32; available online,
   www.marxists.org (27 December 2013); Trotsky, *In Defense of
   Marxism*, pp. 114, 115; Paul Le Blanc, 'From Revolutionary Intellectual
   to Conservative Master-thinker: The Anti-Democratic Odyssey of
   James Burnham', *Left History*, iii/1 (Spring/Summer 1995), pp. 49–81;
   David Cotterill, ed., *The Serge-Trotsky Papers: Correspondence and Other
   Writings between Victor Serge and Leon Trotsky* (London, 1994).

21 Victor Serge, *Memoirs of a Revolutionary* (New York, 2012), p. 156.

22 'Intellectual Ex-radicals and World Reaction', in *Writings of Leon Trotsky,
   1938–39*, ed. Naomi Allen and George Breitman (New York, 1974),
   p. 196.

23 'The Beginning of the End', in *Writings of Leon Trotsky, 1936–37*,
   pp. 328–9.

24 Bertram D. Wolfe, *Diego Rivera: His Life and Times* (New York, 1939),
   pp. 401, 402; Bertram D. Wolfe, *A Life in Two Centuries: An
   Autobiography* (New York, 1981), p. 304.

25 Bertram D. Wolfe, *The Fabulous Life of Diego Rivera* (New York, 1963),
   pp. 7, 385; Dora Apel, 'Diego Rivera and the Left: The Destruction
   and Recreation of the Rockefeller Center Mural', *Left History*, vi/1
   (1999), p. 58.

26 Jean van Heijenoort, *With Trotsky in Exile: From Prinkipo to Coyoacán*
   (Cambridge, MA, 1978), pp. 134–8; 'The Diego Rivera Affair', *Writings
   of Leon Trotsky, 1938–39*, pp. 267–97; Hansen, 'With Trotsky in
   Coyoacán', in Trotsky, *My Life*, p. xxi.

27 Ralph E. Shikes, *The Indignant Eye: The Artist as Social Critic* (Boston,
   MA, 1969), pp. 379, 380, 381; Van Heijenoort, *With Trotsky in Exile*,
   p. 126; Bertrand M. Patenaude, *Trotsky: Downfall of a Revolutionary*
   (New York, 2009), p. 163.

28 Esteban Volkov [Volkow], 'Reflections on the Legacy of Leon Trotsky'
   [presented at conference on 'The Legacy of Leon Trotsky and U.S.
   Trotskyism', 25–7 July 2008, at Fordham University], *Labor Standard*,
   http://laborstandard.org (accessed 28 December, 2013); additional
   sources used here are Victor Serge and Natalia Sedova Trotsky,
   The Life and Death of Leon Trotsky (New York, 1975), pp. 256–61;
   and Patenaude, *Trotsky*, pp. 1–11, 252–61.

29 Jake Cooper, 'Memories of Trotsky' [1988], http://web.archive.org/
web/ 20091026191742/http://www.geocities .com/youth4sa/
trotsky-cooper.html (accessed 25 January 2014); Wilmers,
The Eitingons, pp. 303–4; Andrew and Mitrokhin, *The Sword and
the Shield*, p. 87.

30 Vittorio Vidali, *Diary of the Twentieth Congress of the Communist Party
of the Soviet Union* (Westport, CT, 1984), p. 155.

31 For example: Isaac Don Levine, *The Mind of an Assassin* (New York,
1959); Serge and Sedova Trotsky, *The Life and Death of Leon Trotsky*,
pp. 245–79; Patenaude, *Trotsky*, pp. 230–92.

32 Volkov [Volkow], 'Reflections on the Legacy of Leon Trotsky'
(accessed 28 December 2013); also see Jo Tuckman, 'Trotsky's
Murder Remembered by Grandson 72 Years On', *The Guardian*,
19 August 2012, www.theguardian.com (accessed
28 December 2013).

33 Joseph Hansen, 'With Trotsky to the End', in *Leon Trotsky: The Man
and His Work* (New York, 1969), p. 17; Serge and Sedova Trotsky,
The Life and Death of Leon Trotsky, pp. 267–8.

6 Afterlife

1 Natalia Sedova, 'How It Happened', *Leon Trotsky, the Man and his
Work: Reminiscences and Appraisals* (New York, 1969), p. 39; Enrique
Soto-Pérez-de-Celis, 'The Death of Leon Trotsky', *Neurosurgery*,
XLVII/2 (August 2010), pp. 419–20.

2 Lillian Pollak, *The Sweetest Dream: Love, Lies, Assassination and Hope,
A Novel of the Thirties* (Bloomington, IN, 2009), pp. 337–9.

3 Joseph Hansen, 'With Trotsky to the End', in *Leon Trotsky, the Man
and his Work*, p. 24.

4 Charles Cornell, 'With Trotsky in Mexico', in *Leon Trotsky, the Man
and his Work*, p. 67.

5 Paul Siegel, 'The Last Years of Stalin and Trotsky', *Socialist Action*
(March 2001), http://saction.igc.org; Nikita Khruschev, *Khrushchev
Remembers* (Boston, MA, 1970), p. 601.

6 'Trotsky's Testament', in Leon Trotsky, *Writings in Exile*, ed. Kunal
Chattopadhyay and Paul Le Blanc (London, 2012), pp. 200–221.

7 'Imperialist War and World Revolution', in *Documents of the Fourth International: The Formative Years (1933–40)*, ed. Will Reissner (New York, 1973), p. 344.

8 Among sources for this analysis are Gabriel Kolko, *The Politics of War: The World and United States Foreign Policy, 1943–1945* (New York, 1968); Fernando Claudin, *The Communist Movement, From Comintern to Cominform*, 2 vols (New York, 1975); Ernest Mandel, *The Meaning of the Second World War* (London, 1986); Donald Sassoon, *One Hundred Years of Socialism: The West European Left in the Twentieth Century* (New York, 1996); and Geoff Eley, *Forging Democracy: The History of the Left in Europe, 1850–2000* (New York, 2002).

9 Maurice Crouzet, *The European Renaissance since 1945* (London, 1970), pp. 89–90.

10 On u.s. imperialism see William Appleman Williams, *The Tragedy of American Diplomacy*, 50th Anniversary Edition (New York, 2009); Harry Magdoff, *Imperialism: From the Colonial Age to the Present* (New York, 1978); and William Blum, *Killing Hope: u.s. Military and cia Interventions since World War ii* (Monroe, me, 1995). The confrontation of the 'superpowers' at the height of the Cold War is described by C. Wright Mills, in his early polemic *The Causes of World War Three* (New York, 1960). The Cold War's history is traced in innumerable works, including Jeremy Isaacs, *Cold War, An Illustrated History, 1945–1991* (Boston, ma, 1998) and, including its aftermath, Walter Lafeber, *America, Russia and the Cold War, 1945–2006* (New York, 2006).

11 Perry Anderson, *Considerations on Western Marxism* (London, 1979), p. 98.

12 Pierre Frank, in *The Fourth International: The Long March of the Trotskyists* (London, 1979), lightly covers some of this ground, and Robert J. Alexander's massive *International Trotskyism, 1929–1985: A Documented Analysis of the Movement* (Durham, nc, 1991) makes a bigger dent. A more detailed yet hardly complete exploration of u.s. Trotskyism can be found in George Breitman, Paul Le Blanc and Alan Wald, *Trotskyism in the United States: Historical Essays and Reconsiderations* (Atlantic Highlands, nj, 1996). An outstanding journal from the uk which over the years has offered considerable material on Trotskyist history is *Revolutionary History* (www.marxists.org, accessed

30 December 2013), and also invaluable is *Encyclopedia of Trotskyism On-Line* (www.marxists.org, accessed 30 December 2013). A sample of Trotskyist influence in the global youth radicalization of the 1960s is Tariq Ali, ed., *The New Revolutionaries: A Handbook of the International Radical Left* (New York, 1969).

13 See Manfred B. Steger, *Globalization: A Very Short Introduction* (Oxford, 2003); Manfred B. Steger and Ravi K. Roy, *Neoliberalism: A Very Short Introduction* (Oxford, 2010); Paul Mason, *Why It's Still Kicking Off Everywhere* (London, 2013); and Luke Cooper and Simon Hardy, *Beyond Capitalism? The Future of Radical Politics* (Winchester, 2012).

14 Irving Howe, *Leon Trotsky* (New York, 1978), p. 192; Joshua Rubenstein, *Leon Trotsky: A Revolutionary's Life* (New Haven, CT, 2011), pp. 206, 209.

15 See Paul Le Blanc, *From Marx to Gramsci: A Reader in Revolutionary Marxist Politics* (Atlantic Highlands, NJ, 1996) and Ernest Mandel, *The Place of Marxism in History* (Atlantic Highlands, NJ, 1996). Among sympathetic efforts to briefly define specifics of 'Trotskyism' are Daniel Bensaid, 'Trotsky, Revolution, and the Constitution of Original "Trotskyism"', at http://danielbensaid.org (accessed 30 December 2013); and Alex Callinicos, *Trotskyism* (Minneapolis, MN, 1990), pp. 6–22.

16 C. Wright Mills, *The Marxists* (New York, 1961), p. 35.

Further Reading

Alexander, Robert J., *International Trotskyism, 1929–1985: A Documented Analysis of the Movement* (Durham, NC, 1991)

Ali, Tariq, and Phil Evans, *Leon Trotsky: An Illustrated Introduction* (Chicago, 2013)

Berger, Joseph, *Shipwreck of a Generation* (London, 1971)

Breitman, George, and collaborators, eds, *The Writings of Leon Trotsky, 1929–1940* (New York, 1973–9), 14 vols

Brotherstone, Terry, and Paul Dukes, eds, *The Trotsky Reappraisal* (Edinburgh, 1992)

Broué, Pierre, *Trotsky* (Paris, 1988)

Carr, E. H., *The Russian Revolution from Lenin to Stalin, 1917–1929* (New York, 2004)

Chamberlin, William H., *The Russian Revolution, 1917–1921* (Princeton, NJ, 1987), 2 vols

Chattopadhyay, Kunal, *The Marxism of Leon Trotsky* (Kolkata, 2006)

—, and Paul Le Blanc, eds, *Leon Trotsky, Writings in Exile* (London, 2012)

Deutscher, Isaac, *The Prophet Armed, Trotsky, 1879–1921* (London, 2004)

—, *The Prophet Unarmed, Trotsky, 1921–1929* (London, 2004)

—, *The Prophet Outcast, Trotsky, 1929–1940* (London, 2004)

Dunn, Bill and Hugo Radice, eds, *100 Years of Permanent Revolution, Results and Prospects* (London, 2006)

Feeley, Dianne, Paul Le Blanc and Thomas Twiss, *Leon Trotsky on the Organizational Principles of the Revolutionary Party* (Chicago, 2014)

Frank, Pierre, *The Fourth International: The Long March of the Trotskyists* (London, 1979)

Geary, Rick, *Trotsky: A Graphic Biography* (New York, 2009)

Hallas, Duncan, *Trotsky's Marxism and Other Essays* (Chicago, 2003)

Høidal, Oddvar K., *Trotsky in Norway: Exile, 1935–1937* (DeKalb, IL, 2013)

Howe, Irving, *Leon Trotsky* (New York, 1978)

King, David, *Trotsky: A Photographic Biography* (Oxford, 1986)

Knei-Paz, Baruch, *The Social and Political Thought of Leon Trotsky* (New York, 1980)

Le Blanc, Paul, *From Marx to Gramsci: A Reader in Revolutionary Marxist Politics* (Amherst, NY, 1996)

Lewin, Moshe, *The Soviet Century* (London, 2005)

Löwy, Michael, *The Politics of Combined and Uneven Development: Trotsky's Theory of Permanent Revolution* (London, 1981)

Mandel, Ernest, *Trotsky as Alternative* (London, 1995)

Mayer, Arno J., *The Furies: Violence and Terror in the French and Russian Revolutions* (Princeton, NJ, 2000)

Patenaude, Bertrand M. *Trotsky: Downfall of a Revolutionary* (New York, 2009)

Rogovin, Vadim Z., *1937: Stalin's Year of Terror* (Oak Park, MI, 1998)

—, *Stalin's Terror of 1937–1938* (Oak Park, MI, 2009)

Rosmer, Alfred, *Moscow Under Lenin* (New York, 1972)

Rubenstein, Joshua, *Leon Trotsky, A Revolutionary's Life* (New Haven, CT, 2011)

Serge, Victor, *Memoirs of a Revolutionary* (New York, 2012)

—, and Natalia Sedova Trotsky, *The Life and Death of Leon Trotsky* (New York, 1975)

Suny, Ronald G., *The Soviet Experiment: Russia, the USSR, and the Successor States*, 2nd edn (New York, 2010)

Ticktin, Hillel and Michael Cox, eds, *The Ideas of Leon Trotsky* (London, 1995)

Trotsky, Leon *History of the Russian Revolution* (Chicago, 2008)

—, *My Life* (New York, 1970)

—, *The Permanent Revolution and Tasks and Prospects* (London, 2007)

—, *The Revolution Betrayed* (Mineola, NY, 2004)

Twiss, Thomas, *Trotsky and the Problem of Soviet Bureaucracy* (Boston and Leiden, 2014)

Van Heijenoort, Jean, *With Trotsky in Exile, From Prinkipo to Coyoacán* (Cambridge, MA, 1978)

Wade, Rex, *The Russian Revolution, 1917*, 2nd edn (New York, 2005)

Online Resources

Marxist Internet Archive, which houses the Trotsky Internet Archive
and the Encyclopedia of Trotskyism On-Line (ETOL)
www.marxists.org, www.marxists.org/archive/trotsky and
www.marxists.org/history/etol

'Trotsky and Permanent Revolution', one of several related slideshows
at the Get Political Now website
http://getpoliticalnow.com/political-lives

'TrotskyanaNet' website of Wolfgang and Petra Lubitz
www.trotskyana.net

Revolutionary History
www.revolutionaryhistory.co.uk and
www.marxists.org/history/etol/revhist/main

Novels

Delahunt, Meghan, *In the Casa Azul: A Novel of Revolution and Betrayal*
(New York, 2001)
Kingsolver, Barbara, *The Lacuna* (New York, 2009)
Padua, Leonardo, *The Man Who Loved Dogs* (New York, 2014)
Pollak, Lillian, *The Sweetest Dream: Love, Lies, Assassination and Hope*,
repr. (New York, 2009)
Serge, Victor, *Midnight in the Century* (London, 1982)

Acknowledgements

George Breitman (with collaborators Sarah Lovell, Naomi Allen, George Shriver and others) made so many of Trotsky's writings available in English, and his thoughtfulness, integrity and comradeship helped many to understand the meaning of those writings. I dedicate this work to his memory, with deep thanks.

Friends Tom Twiss, Kunal Chattopadhyay and Michael Löwy have contributed much to my understanding of Trotsky. For helpful feedback as I prepared drafts of this book, thanks to Ian Birchall, Nancy Ferrari, Peter Hudis, Michael Löwy, John Riddell, Andrew Ryder, Jon Sherry and the especially sharp-eyed George Shriver.

Trotsky's grandson, Esteban Volkow, and our mutual friend Danny Laird, offered invaluable help in more ways than one, for which I am deeply grateful.

Thanks also to the publisher Michael Leaman and others at Reaktion Books for helping to bring this book into being.

Regarding illustrations, help from Susannah Jayes at Reaktion Books was essential. I am especially appreciative to the following for providing images: David King Collection, London; Esteban Volkow and the Museo Casa de León Trotsky; Christie McDonald, who graciously gave permission to reproduce the portrait of Trotsky painted by her mother, Dorothy Eisner; the late Carol McAllister. Tom Twiss and most especially Jonah McAllister-Erickson rendered wondrous assistance in the scanning of images. Crucial assistance at a decisive moment was supplied by Professor Miranda Hall and Chelsey Docherty of the Graphic and Communication Design Department at La Roche College.

PERMISSIONS

For permission to reprint the excerpt from Victor Serge's poem 'Confessions' (from his collection *Resistance*), translation copyright © by James Brook, my grateful thanks to City Lights Books, San Francisco, California. My quotation from N. N. Sukhanov, *The Russian Revolution, 1917: A Personal Record* is © 1984 copyright Princeton University Press, and used with permission.

Photo Acknowledgements

The author and the publishers wish to express their thanks to the below sources of illustrative material and /or permission to reproduce it.

© 2015 Banco de México Diego Rivera Frida Kahlo Museums Trust, Mexico, D.F. / DACS: p. 14; Alex Buchman: p. 6; Corbis: pp. 27, 33, 41, 44 (Hulton-Deutsch Collection), 103 (Bettmann); Getty Images: pp. 19, 76 top (Fine Art Images / Heritage Images), 76 bottom (Sovfoto / UIG via Getty Images), 83 (Hulton Archive), 92 (Planet News Archives / SSPL); Houghton Library, Harvard University, Cambridge, Massachusetts, reproduced with kind permission of Christie McDonald, p. 188; David King Collection, London: pp. 11, 36, 53, 58, 60, 62 top right, 66, 96, 114, 121, 149; Library of Congress, Washington, DC: p. 128; Carol McAllister: p. 181; Thomas Twiss: p. 111; Esteban Volkow and the Museo Casa de León Trotsky: p. 91 top left; Raya Dunayevskaya Collection, Walter P. Reuther Library, Archives of Labor and Urban Affairs, Wayne State University: p. 131.